True Stories
1A

Sandra Heyer

True Stories: Level 1A, Silver Edition

Copyright © 2019 by Pearson Education, Inc.
All rights reserved.

No part of this publication may be reproduced, stored in a retrieval system, or transmitted in any form or by any means, electronic, mechanical, photocopying, recording, or otherwise, without the prior permission of the publisher.

Pearson Education, 221 River Street, Hoboken, NJ 07030

Staff Credits: The people who made up the *True Stories: Level 1A, Silver Edition* team, representing content creation, design, manufacturing, marketing, multimedia, project management, publishing, rights management, and testing, are Pietro Alongi, Tracey Cataldo, Dave Dickey, Warren Fischbach, Lucy Hart, Gosia Jaros-White, Barry Katzen, Linda Moser, Dana Pinter, Paula Van Ells, Joseph Vella, and Peter West.

Text design and layout: Don Williams
Composition: Page Designs International
Project supervision: Bernard Seal
Contributing editor: Bernard Seal

Cover images: *(from top to bottom)* Paul Knowles/Shutterstock; PBO Photography/Shutterstock; lydiarei/Shutterstock; danm12/Shutterstock; Magnus Johansson/123RF; *(silver edition badge)* deepstock/Shutterstock.
Illustrations: Don Martinetti, Andrés Morales, and Aptara

Library of Congress Cataloging-in-Publication Data

A catalog record for the print edition is available from the Library of Congress.

Printed in the United States of America

ISBN-10: 0-13-5177901
ISBN-13: 978-0-13-517790-7

7 2020

CONTENTS

Introduction iv
Acknowledgments vii
From the Author ix

UNIT 1	The Big TVs 2
UNIT 2	The Man in the Blue Car 6
UNIT 3	Mr. Venezuela 10
UNIT 4	Hot Soup 14
UNIT 5	Give Me the Money! 18
UNIT 6	Looking for Love 22
UNIT 7	License, Please 26
UNIT 8	Election Day 30
UNIT 9	The Best Doctor 34
UNIT 10	Larry's Favorite Shirt 38
UNIT 11	What a Boy! What a Toy! 42
UNIT 12	The Flying Lesson 46
UNIT 13	Two Happy Men 50
UNIT 14	Speed 54
UNIT 15	The Kind Waitress 58
UNIT 16	Grandfather Hada's Favorite Soup 62
UNIT 17	No More Housework! 66
UNIT 18	The Bottle 70
UNIT 19	Whose Money Is It? 74
UNIT 20	The Gold Ring 78

Key to Guessed Answers 83
Dictation Preparation Directions 83
Answer Key 85
Credits 95

INTRODUCTION

TRUE STORIES, SILVER EDITION

The Silver Edition of *True Stories* is a five-level reading series. The series is appropriate for beginning to high-intermediate learners of English as a Second or Foreign Language. The Silver Edition consists of revised editions of six of the highly successful and popular *True Stories in the News* books that have provided entertaining stories and effective reading skill instruction for many years. In fact, the first book in that series was published over twenty-five years ago (hence the title "Silver" Edition). The *True Stories* series has been going strong ever since.

NEW IN THE SILVER EDITION

- **New and updated stories.** Some stories have been updated, and some have been replaced with fresh new readings that have been thoroughly classroom-tested before making it into print. All of the readings that have proven to be favorites of students and teachers over the years have been retained.

- **A colorful new design.** Originally published solely in black and white, the new edition has a new full-color design with colorful new photos. The color design makes the readings even more inviting, and the color photos that accompany the readings enhance understanding and enjoyment of the stories.

- **A uniform unit structure.** The books in the series have been given a consistent unit structure that runs across all six books. This predictable structure makes it easy for teachers to teach the series at different levels and for students to progress seamlessly from one level to the next.

- **Audio recordings of every reading.** Every story in the series has been recorded and made available online for students or teachers to download.

- **Online Answer Keys and To the Teacher notes.** In addition to being in the back of the books, as they were in the previous editions, the Answer Keys are now also online as downloadable pdfs. The To the Teacher notes that were previously in the back of the books, however, are now only online. This section provides additional information about the stories and teaching tips. Additional practice activities are also now available online.

THE APPROACH

The underlying premise in this series has always been that when second language learners are engaged in a pleasurable reading experience in the second language, then language learning will take place effortlessly and effectively. The formula is simple: Offer students a true story that fascinates and surprises them. Have them read and enjoy the story. Focus their attention on some useful vocabulary in the story. Confirm that they fully understand the story with reading comprehension exercises. Develop reading skills that progress from basic to more complex. Finally, use the content and the topic of the story to engage in discussion and writing tasks, from tightly structured to more open-ended.

UNIT COMPONENTS

Pre-Reading

Each unit begins with a pre-reading task that piques students' curiosity about the content of the story. Students' attention is drawn to the art that accompanies the reading and the title of the reading as they predict what the story is going to be about.

Reading

The readings are short enough to be read by the students in class; at the lower levels, the stories can be read in minutes. As the levels become higher, the readings do become longer and more challenging. Still, even at the highest levels, each reading and the exercises immediately following it can be completed in one class meeting.

Post-Reading

While there is some variation in the post-reading activities, the following are in all six books:

- **Vocabulary.** Useful key vocabulary items are selected from the readings for presentation and practice. The vocabulary activities vary from unit to unit, and the number of vocabulary items and the extent of the practice increases from level to level.

- **Comprehension.** At least two different comprehension tasks follow the vocabulary section. The exercises have descriptive titles, such as Understanding the Main Ideas, Remembering Details, or Understanding Cause and Effect, so that teachers and students know which cognitive skills are being applied. The exercises have a great deal of variety, keeping students engaged and motivated.

- **Discussion.** Having read and studied the stories, students are encouraged to discuss some aspect arising from the story. Even at the lowest level, students are given simple tasks that will give them the opportunity to talk in pairs, in small groups, or as a whole class.

- **Writing.** The final section of each unit has students produce a short piece of writing related to the reading. Often the writing task derives directly from the Discussion, in which case the title of the section is Discussion/Writing. The writing tasks are level-appropriate and vary in complexity depending on student proficiency. The tasks are not intended to be graded. They simply provide a final opportunity for students to engage with the topic of the reading and deepen their understanding and enjoyment of the story.

TRUE STORIES, LEVEL 1A

True Stories, Level 1A is the lowest level in the Silver Edition of the *True Stories* series. It is intended for beginning learners of English. It consists of 20 four-page units, each with the following distinguishing features:

- The pre-reading task has students listen to each story while looking at illustrations that recreate the story's narrative.

- Each story has an average length of just over 200 words.

- There is an overlap in level with *True Stories* 1B so that students can smoothly transition from this book to the next book in the series.

- The stories are told in the simple present, present progressive, and future tenses, with occasional use of the past tense.

- Writing exercises are dictations, sentence completions, and composition of single sentences.

ACKNOWLEDGMENTS

I would like to thank

- the many teachers whose invaluable feedback helped me assess how the stories and exercises were working outside the small sphere of my own classroom. If I were to list you all by name, this acknowledgments section would go on for pages. I would like to thank three colleagues in particular: legendary teacher Peggy Miles, who introduced me to the world of English language teaching; Sharron Bassano, whose innovative techniques for teaching beginning-level students informed my own approach; and Jorge Islas Martinez, whose enthusiasm and dedication remain a constant inspiration;

- my students, who shared personal stories that became the examples for the discussion and writing exercises;

- the people in the stories who supplied details that were not in news sources: Twyla Thompson, John Koehler, Dorothy Peckham, Chi Hsii Tsui, Margaret Patrick, Trish Moore and Rhonda Gill (grandmother and mother of Desiree), Friendship Force participants, Natalie Garibian, Mirsada Buric, and the late Irvin Scott;

- the teachers and editors who made important contributions at different stages of development to the previous editions of these books and whose influence can still be seen throughout this new edition: Allen Ascher, John Barnes, Karen Davy, Joanne Dresner, Nancy Hayward, Stacey Hunter, Penny LaPorte, Laura LeDrean, Françoise Leffler, Linda Moser, Dana Klinek Pinter, Mary Perrotta Rich, Debbie Sistino, and Paula Van Ells;

- Rachel Hayward and Megan Hohenstein, who assisted in piloting and researching new material for the Silver Edition;

- the team at Pearson, whose experienced hands skillfully put together all the moving pieces in the preparation of this Silver Edition: Pietro Alongi, Tracey Cataldo, Warren Fischbach, Lucy Hart, Gosia Jaros-White, Linda Moser, Dana Pinter, Joseph Vella, and Peter West;

- copyeditor and fact checker, Kate Smyres; and proofreader, Ann Dickson;

- editor extraordinaire Françoise Leffler, who lent her expertise to *True Stories* levels 4 and 5;

- Bernard Seal at Page Designs International, who guided this project from start to finish with dedication, creativity, pragmatism, and the occasional "crazy"—but brilliant—idea;

- Don Williams at Page Designs International, whose talent for design is evident on every page; and

- my husband, John Hajdu Heyer, who read the first draft of every story I've considered for the *True Stories* series. The expression on his face as he read told me whether or not the story was a keeper. He didn't know that. Now he does.

FROM THE AUTHOR

Dear Teachers and Students,

This new edition of *True Stories* is the Silver Edition because it celebrates an anniversary—it has been more than 25 years since the first *True Stories* book was published. The way we get our news has changed a lot over the years, but some things have remained the same: Fascinating stories are in the news every day, and the goal of the *True Stories* series is still to bring the best of them to you.

The question students ask most often about these stories is *Are they true?* The answer is *yes*—to the best of my knowledge, these stories are true. I've fact-checked stories by contacting reporters, photojournalists, and research librarians all over the world. I've even called some of the people in the stories to be sure I have the facts right.

Once I'm as sure as I can be that a story is true, the story has to pass one more test. My students read the story, and after they finish reading, they give each story one, two, or three stars. They take this responsibility seriously; they know that only the top-rated stories will become part of the *True Stories* reading series.

I hope that you, too, think these are three-star stories. And I hope that reading them encourages you to share your own stories, which are always the most amazing true stories of all.

Sandra Heyer

UNIT 1

1 PRE-READING

Look at the pictures. Listen to your teacher tell the story.

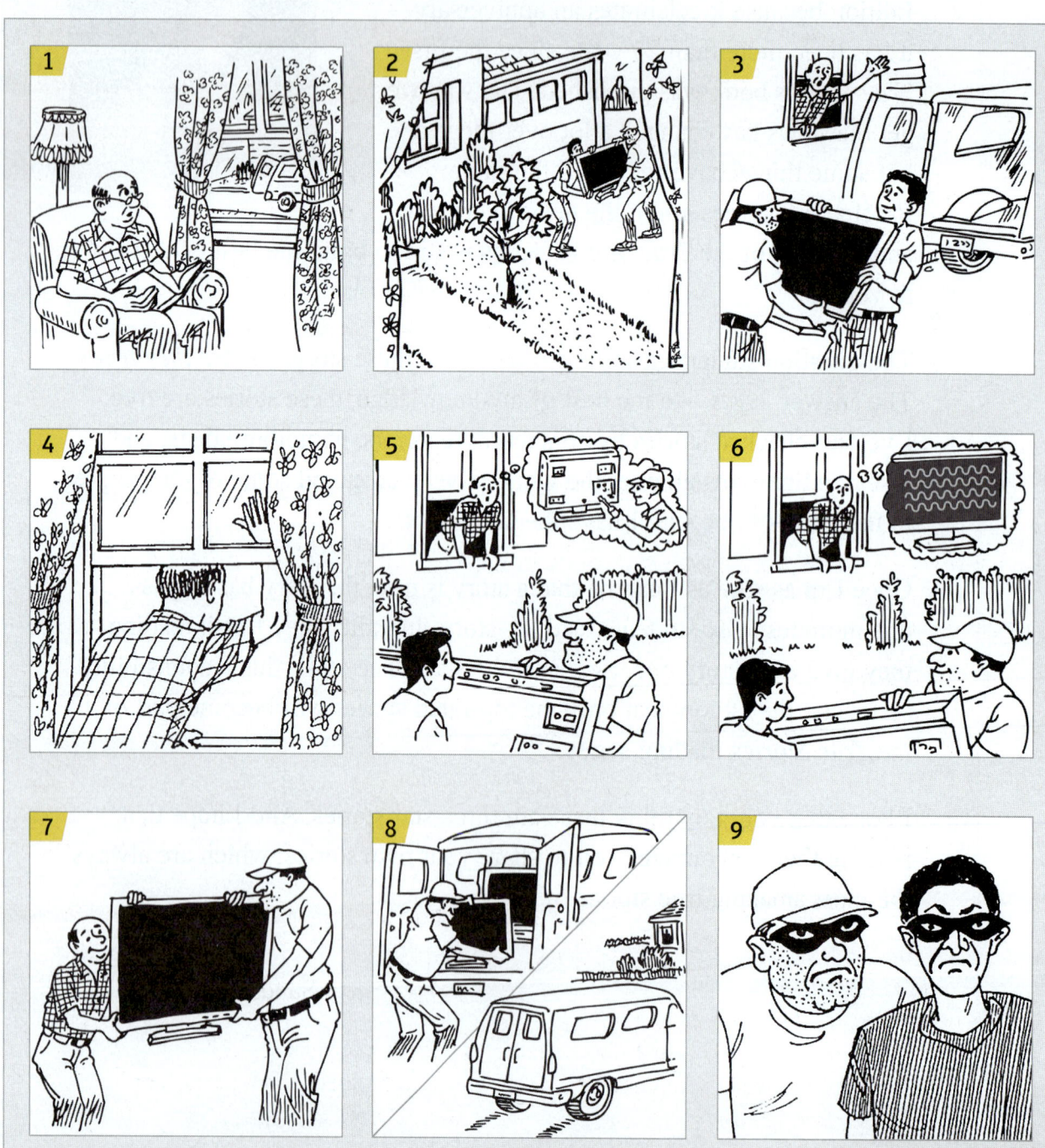

The Big TVs

Jim is at home in his living room. He is reading in a chair near the window. He hears a noise outside, so he gets up to take a look.

When Jim looks out the window, he sees two men. They are in his neighbor's driveway. They are carrying a big TV. They are carrying the TV to a van.

Jim opens the window. "Hey!" he says to the two men. "Are you TV repairmen?"

"Yes," the men answer.

"Are you going to fix that TV?" Jim asks.

"Yes," the men answer again.

"My TV is broken," Jim tells the men. "Can you take my TV, too?"

"Sure," the men say. "We can take your TV."

Jim gives the men his TV. The men put the two TVs in the van and drive away.

Jim never sees his TV again.

The two men aren't TV repairmen. They are robbers.

2 VOCABULARY

Match the words and the pictures. Write your answer on the line.

| drive away | driveway | carry | fix | neighbor | robber |

1. _____driveway_____   2. _____   3. _____

4. _____   5. _____   6. _____

3 COMPREHENSION

REMEMBERING DETAILS

Which sentence is correct? Circle *a* or *b*.

1. a. Jim is at home in his living room.
   b. Jim is at home in his kitchen.

2. a. Jim sees two cars in his neighbor's driveway.
   b. Jim sees two men in his neighbor's driveway.

3. a. The men are carrying a big table.
   b. The men are carrying a big TV.

4. a. Jim asks the men, "Are you going to fix that TV?"
   b. Jim asks the men, "Are you going to watch that TV?"

5. a. Jim tells the men, "My TV is broken."
   b. Jim tells the men, "My TV is old."

6. a. The men put the TVs in the van and pay Jim $50.
   b. The men put the TVs in the van and drive away.

4 Unit 1

REVIEWING THE STORY

Write the correct word on the line.

Jim sees two men in his ____*neighbor's*____ driveway. The men are
                              1.
_____ a big TV. Jim thinks the men are TV _____.
       2.   3.
He gives them his _____. Jim never sees his TV again because the
                        4.
men are _____.
              5.

4 DISCUSSION / WRITING

Jim sees two men in his neighbor's driveway. They are carrying a TV. Jim doesn't call 911. He thinks the robbers are TV repairmen.

A Imagine this: You see a man at your neighbor's home. The man is carrying a TV. The man is a robber. You are sure of it. You call 911. The 911 operator asks you questions. Write your answers on the lines.

OPERATOR: What's your emergency?

YOU: _____

OPERATOR: What's the address?

YOU: _____

OPERATOR: What's your name?

YOU: _____

OPERATOR: What is the man wearing?

YOU: _____

OPERATOR: How tall is he?

YOU: _____

OPERATOR: How old is he?

YOU: _____

OPERATOR: OK. The police are on their way. Stay away from the man.

B Read the questions and answers aloud with a partner.

C If you have a true story about a robbery, tell the class.

UNIT 2

1 PRE-READING

Look at the pictures. Listen to your teacher tell the story.

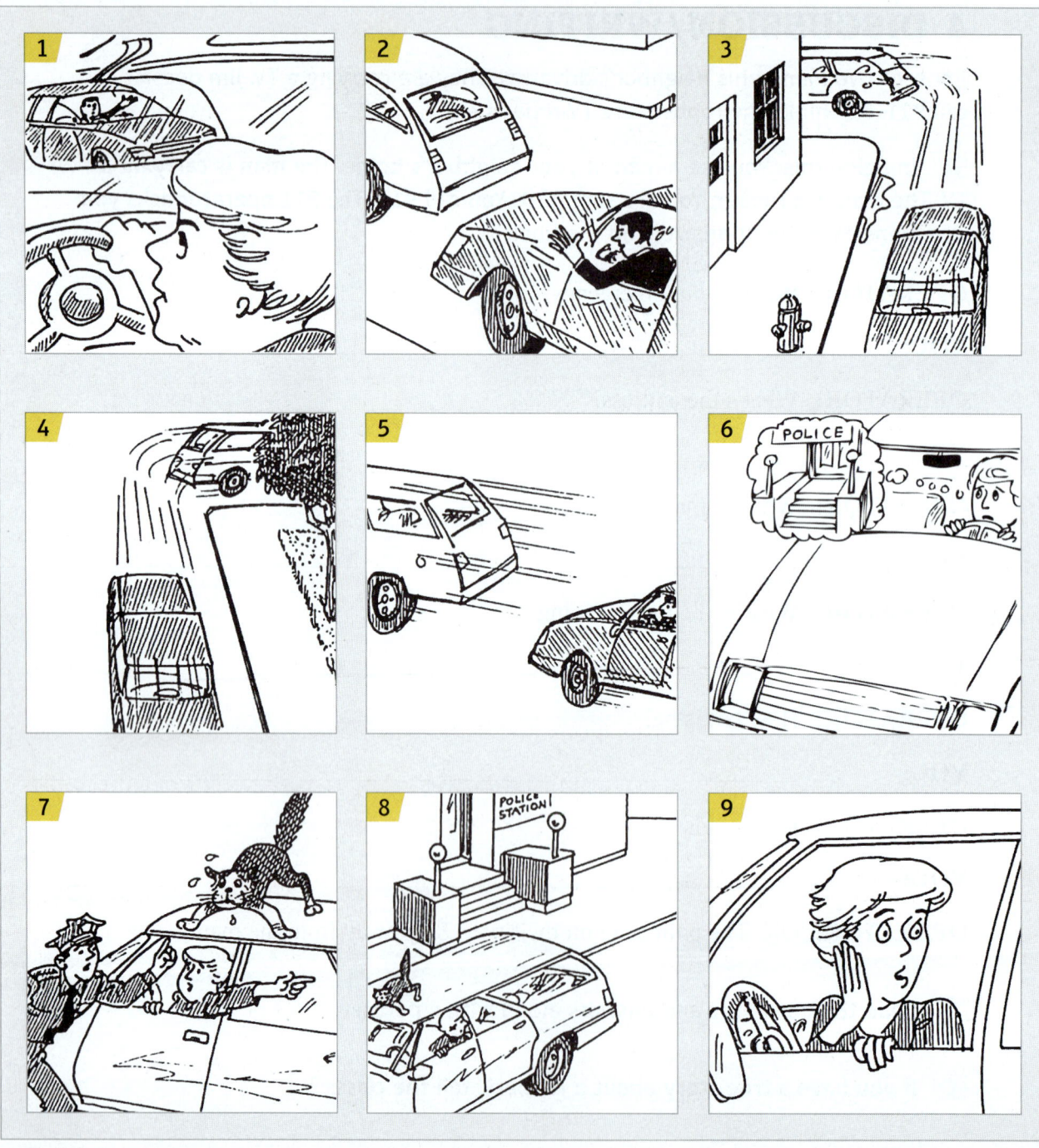

6

The Man in the Blue Car

Mrs. Thompson is driving her car. She looks in the rearview mirror. A blue car is behind her. A man is driving the blue car.

The man in the blue car waves at Mrs. Thompson. He is saying something, but Mrs. Thompson can't hear him.

Mrs. Thompson turns left. The man in the blue car turns left, too.

Mrs. Thompson turns right. The man in the blue car turns right, too.

Mrs. Thompson drives fast. The man in the blue car drives fast, too.

Mrs. Thompson is afraid of the man in the blue car. Why is he waving at her? What is he saying? Why is he following her? She looks in the rearview mirror again. Is the man in the blue car still behind her? Yes, he is, and now he is turning his headlights on and off! Mrs. Thompson decides to drive to the police station. The man in the blue car follows her.

Mrs. Thompson arrives at the police station and stops her car. A police officer comes to her car and says, "There's a cat on the top of your car!"

Mrs. Thompson's cat is on the top of her car. The cat is *very* afraid.

Mrs. Thompson looks for the man in the blue car, but he is gone. Now Mrs. Thompson understands: The man in the blue car was trying to tell her, "There's a cat on the top of your car!"

2 VOCABULARY

Match the words and the pictures. Write your answer on the line.

afraid   follow   rearview mirror   top of the car   turn left   wave

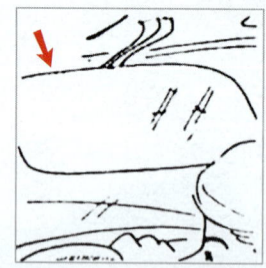

1. _rearview mirror_   2. _____   3. _____

4. _____   5. _____   6. _____

3 COMPREHENSION

REMEMBERING DETAILS

Which sentence is correct? Circle *a* or *b*.

1. a. Mrs. Thompson is driving her truck.
   (b.) Mrs. Thompson is driving her car.

2. a. A blue car is behind her.
   b. A black car is behind her.

3. a. The man in the car follows Mrs. Thompson.
   b. The man in the car likes Mrs. Thompson.

4. a. Mrs. Thompson drives home.
   b. Mrs. Thompson drives to the police station.

5. a. There is a man on the top of Mrs. Thompson's car.
   b. There is a cat on the top of Mrs. Thompson's car.

REVIEWING THE STORY

Write the correct word on the line.

A ____man____ in a blue car follows Mrs. Thompson. Mrs. Thompson
     1.

is _____ of the man. She drives to the _____
     2.   3.

station. A police _____ tells her, "_____ a cat
                       4.   5.

on the top of your car!" Mrs. Thompson looks for the man in the blue car, but he

is _____.
     6.

4 DISCUSSION

Mrs. Thompson is driving with 10 things on the top of her car. Look at the 10 things for 30 seconds. Then close your book. How many things can you remember? With a small group of your classmates, make a list. Which group remembered all 10 things?

5 WRITING

Mrs. Thompson wants to go to the police station. Here are directions to the police station. Some words are missing. Look at the map. Then write the missing words.

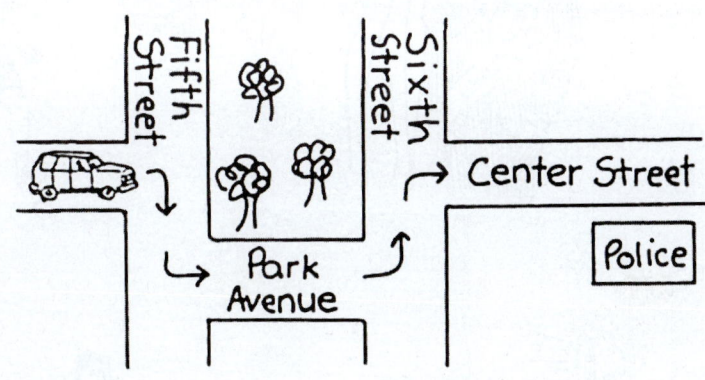

1. Turn ____right____ on Fifth ____Street____.

2. Then turn _____ on _____ Avenue.

3. Now turn _____ on _____ Street.

4. Finally, turn _____ on Center _____.

5. And the police station is on the _____.

UNIT 3

1 PRE-READING

Look at the pictures. Listen to your teacher tell the story.

Mr. Venezuela

Every year, there is a beauty contest in Venezuela. The most beautiful woman is the winner. She is "Miss Venezuela."

Now there is another beauty contest in Venezuela. It is for men only. The most handsome man is the winner. He is "Mr. Venezuela."

Johnny Alvarez, age 23, wants to be Mr. Venezuela, so he is working hard. He is lifting weights, and he is running. He is eating a special diet, too. He is eating only fruit, vegetables, and chicken. He is not eating bread, ice cream, or candy. He wants to look good for the contest.

Why does Johnny want to be Mr. Venezuela? He is a model. "If I am Mr. Venezuela," he says, "I will get a lot of modeling work."

Some men don't like the Mr. Venezuela contest. "Beauty contests are for women," they say. "They are not for men."

But women like the Mr. Venezuela contest. "We like to look at the men," the women say. "The men in Venezuela are the most handsome men in the world."

2 VOCABULARY

Match the words and the pictures. Write your answer on the line.

| beauty contest | lift weights | model | Venezuela | winner |

1. _beauty contest_   2. _____   3. _____

4. _____   5. _____

3 COMPREHENSION

REMEMBERING DETAILS

One word in each sentence is not correct. Find the word and cross it out. Write the correct word.

1. Every ~~month~~, there is a beauty contest in Venezuela. _year_

2. The most intelligent woman is the winner.

3. Now there is another beauty contest for children only.

4. Johnny Alvarez is a doctor.

5. He is eating only fruit, vegetables, and pizza.

6. He is not eating bread, ice cream, or meat.

Unit 3

MAKING CONNECTIONS

Complete the sentences. Write the letter of your answer on the line.

1. Johnny Alvarez is lifting weights and running __b__
2. Johnny wants to be Mr. Venezuela ____
3. Some men don't like the Mr. Venezuela contest ____
4. Women like the Mr. Venezuela contest ____

a. because they think beauty contests are not for men.
b. because he wants to look good for the contest.
c. because he wants to get modeling work.
d. because they like to look at the handsome men.

4 DISCUSSION

A Read the sentences. Check (✓) *YES* or *NO*.

	YES	NO
1. In my country, there are beauty contests for women.	☐	☐
2. In my country, there are beauty contests for men.	☐	☐
3. I think beauty contests for women are a good idea.	☐	☐
4. I think beauty contests for men are a good idea.	☐	☐
5. I like to watch beauty contests.	☐	☐

B Share your answers with your classmates.

5 WRITING

A Imagine this: There is a beauty contest for women on TV. The most beautiful woman is the winner. Will you watch it? Write your answer on the lines below.
Begin:

Yes, I will watch it because . . . OR *No, I won't watch it because . . .*

_____

_____

B Imagine this: There is a beauty contest for men on TV. The most handsome man is the winner. Will you watch it? Write your answer on the lines below.

_____

_____

UNIT 4

1 PRE-READING

Look at the pictures. Listen to your teacher tell the story.

14

Hot Soup

It is lunchtime, and Yuri is hungry. His wife, Olga, is hungry, too. Olga heats up some soup, and they sit down to eat.

"This soup isn't hot," Yuri says.

"It's fine," Olga says. "Eat your soup."

"But it isn't hot," Yuri says. "I like really hot soup."

"Then heat up your soup," Olga says.

Yuri is angry. "I'm going for a walk!" he says. He puts on his coat, hat, and gloves, and he walks out the door. He closes the door with a BANG!

Yuri and Olga live in a small town in Russia. There is a forest near the town. Yuri goes for a walk in the forest. He walks for two hours. Then he feels better. "I'll go home now," he thinks. "I'll tell Olga I'm sorry. Then I'll heat up the soup."

But which way is home? Yuri doesn't know. He is lost. He walks, and walks, and walks. But he can't find his way home.

Yuri is lost in the forest for one week. He eats berries, leaves, and snow. At night he sleeps on the cold ground.

One morning Yuri wakes up and sees some farmworkers. "Help!" he calls to the farmworkers.

The farmworkers take Yuri home to Olga. Yuri is happy to see Olga, and she is happy to see him. Olga heats up some soup and gives it to Yuri. The soup isn't really hot.

"How is the soup?" she asks him.

"It's perfect," he says.

2 VOCABULARY

Match the words and the pictures. Write your answer on the line.

| berries | farmworker | forest | gloves | ground | leaves |

1. _____ground_____ 2. _____ 3. _____

4. _____ 5. _____ 6. _____

3 COMPREHENSION

FINDING INFORMATION

Read each question. Find the answer in the story on the next page and circle it. Write the number of the question above the answer.

1. Where do Yuri and Olga live?
2. What is near the town?
3. How long does Yuri walk in the forest?
4. How does he feel after his walk?
5. What will he tell Olga when he goes home?
6. Why can't Yuri go home?
7. How long is Yuri lost in the forest?
8. What does he eat?
9. Where does he sleep?
10. Who takes Yuri home to Olga?

16 Unit 4

Yuri and Olga live in a small town in Russia. There is a forest near the town. Yuri walks in the forest for two hours. Then he feels better. He decides to go home and tell Olga he is sorry.

Yuri can't go home because he is lost. He is lost in the forest for one week. He eats berries, leaves, and snow. At night he sleeps on the cold ground.

One morning Yuri wakes up and sees some farmworkers. They take him home to Olga.

UNDERSTANDING THE MAIN IDEAS

There are two correct ways to complete each sentence below and one incorrect way. Circle the letters of the two correct answers.

1. Yuri is angry because
   a. he doesn't like soup.
   b. his soup isn't really hot.
   c. Olga tells him, "Heat up your soup."

2. After he walks for two hours, Yuri wants to
   a. tell Olga he is sorry.
   b. take Olga to a restaurant.
   c. heat up his soup.

3. When he is in the forest, Yuri
   a. eats berries, leaves, and snow.
   b. sleeps on the cold ground.
   c. calls for help on his phone.

4. When Yuri comes home, Olga
   a. is angry at him.
   b. is happy to see him.
   c. gives him soup.

4 DISCUSSION / WRITING

Yuri and Olga live in Russia. *Shchi* is a popular soup in Russia. Meat and cabbage are in the soup.

A Answer the questions. Write your answers on the lines.

1. What is your favorite soup? _____
   (You can write the name of the soup in your native language.)

2. What is in the soup? _____

3. Who in your family usually makes the soup? _____

4. How often do you have this soup? _____

B Share your writing in a small group.

UNIT 5

1 PRE-READING

Look at the pictures. Listen to your teacher tell the story.

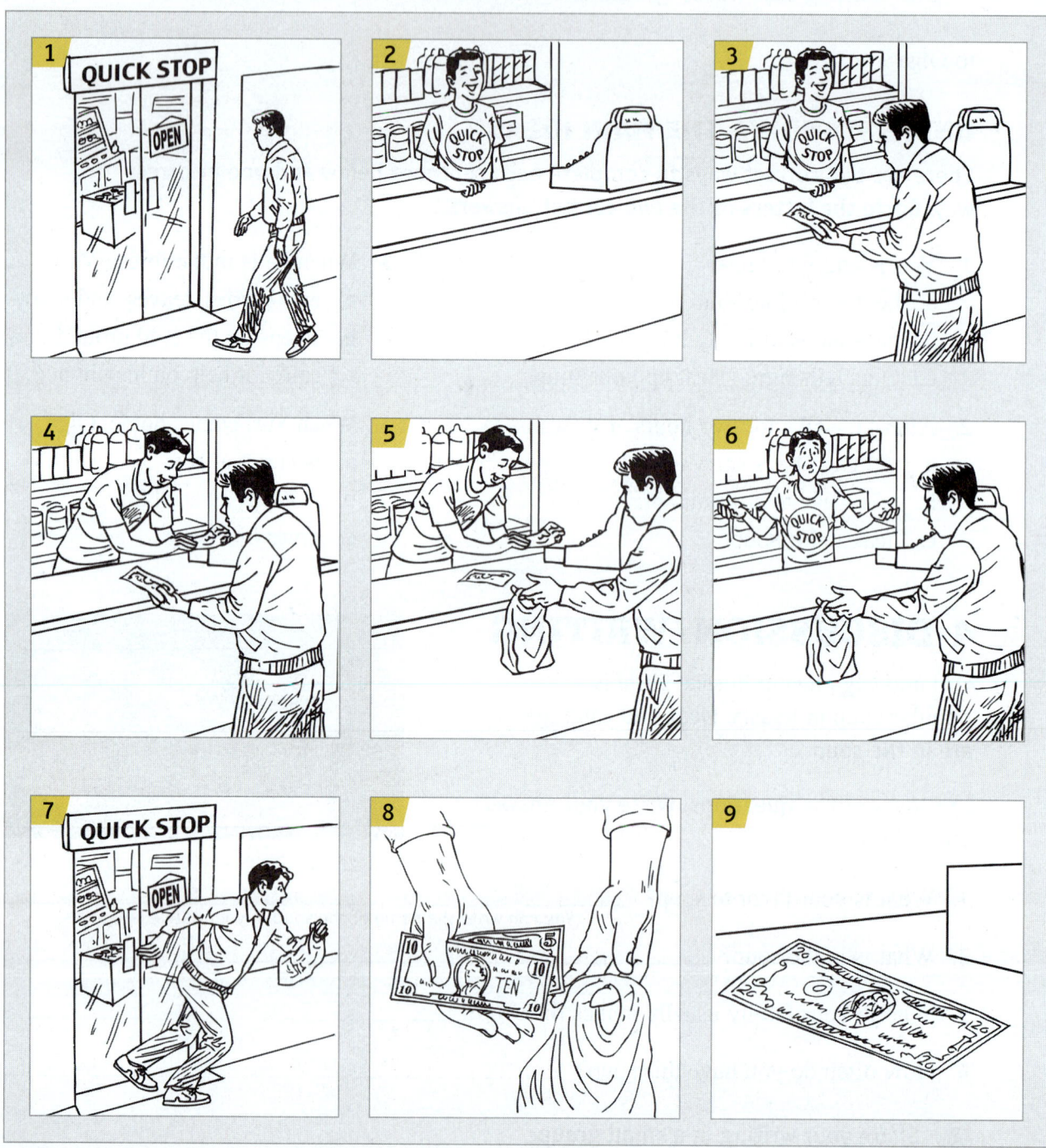

Give Me the Money!

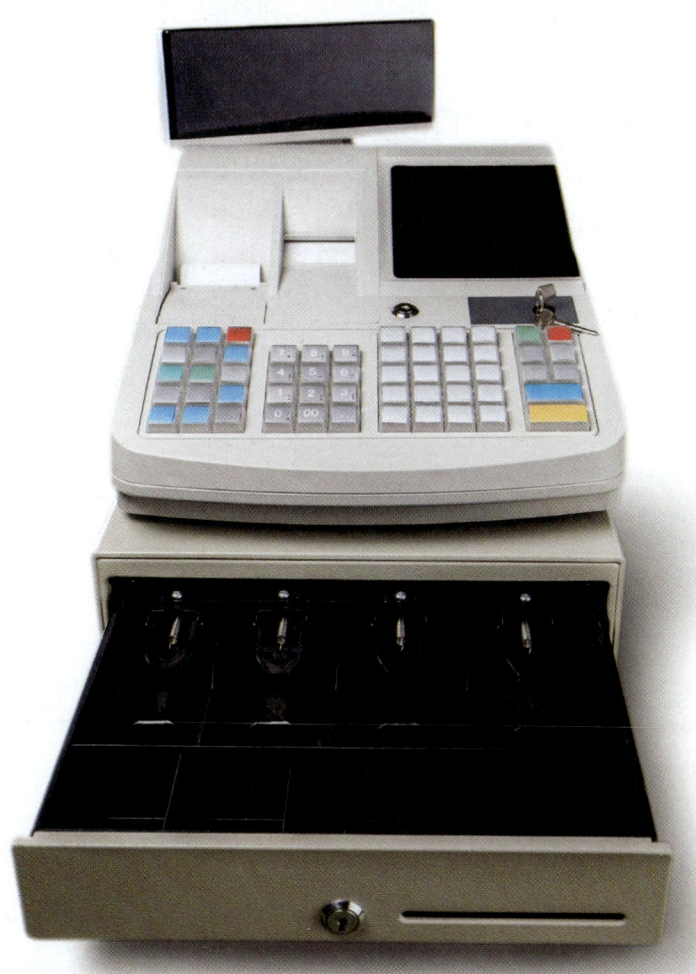

Early one morning, a man walks into a store. It is a small store. It has only one cash register and one cashier.

The man has a $20 bill in his hand. He puts the money on the counter. "Do you have change for a twenty?" the man asks the cashier. "I don't think so," the cashier says. "But I'll look." The cashier opens the cash register.

The man shows the cashier a bag. "Give me all the money!" the man says. "Put it in the bag!"

"But…" the cashier says.

"Give me all the money!" the man says. "Put it in the bag!"

"But…" the cashier says.

"Give me all the money!" the man shouts. "Put it in the bag!"

The man has the bag in his left hand. His right hand is in his pocket. Does he have a gun? The cashier doesn't know.

The cashier puts all the money in the bag. The man takes the bag and runs out of the store.

Later the man opens the bag. What is in it? All the money from the cash register—$15.

What is on the counter at the small store? The man's $20 bill.

2 VOCABULARY

Match the words and the pictures. Write your answer on the line.

| $20 bill | bag | cash register | cashier | counter | pocket |

1. _cash register_   2. _____   3. _____

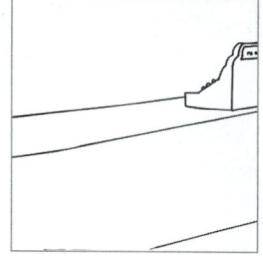  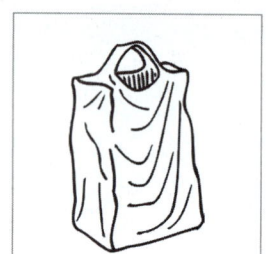

4. _____   5. _____   6. _____

3 COMPREHENSION

REMEMBERING DETAILS

Which sentence is correct? Circle *a* or *b*.

1. a. Late one night, a man walks into a store.
   (b.) Early one morning, a man walks into a store.

2. a. It is a small store.
   b. It is a big store.

3. a. He asks the cashier, "Do you have change for a ten?"
   b. He asks the cashier, "Do you have change for a twenty?"

4. a. "Give me all the money," the man says quietly.
   b. "Give me all the money!" the man shouts.

5. a. The man takes the bag and runs out of the store.
   b. The man takes the bag and walks out of the store.

REVIEWING THE STORY

Write the correct word on the line.

A man walks into a small store. "Do you have ____change____ for a
                                              1.
$20 bill?" he asks the cashier. When the cashier _____ the cash
                                                         2.
register, the man _____ him a bag. "Give me all the
                         3.
_____!" the man shouts. The cashier gives the man
      4.
_____ the money from the cash register—$15. The man runs
      5.
away with the money. He leaves the _____, but he also leaves
                                            6.
his $20 bill on the counter!

4 DISCUSSION

In the story, there is $15 in the cash register at a small store. A man takes the money and runs away. If the police catch him, he will probably go to prison.

A In the United States, how much money is usually in the cash register at a small store? In a small group, take a guess. Write your group's answer here:

$_____

B Imagine this: A man walks into a small store in the United States. He takes all the money in the cash register. Later the police catch him. How long is he in prison? In a small group, take a guess. Write your group's answer here:

_____ years

C Tell the class your group's answers. (The correct answers are on page 83.)

5 WRITING

A Prepare for a dictation. Practice with the sentences below. Follow the directions on page 83.

1. Walk into the store.
2. Put your hand in your pocket.
3. Put money on the counter.
4. Show the cashier a bag.
5. Run out of the store.
6. Open the bag.

B Now close your book. On your own paper, write the sentences as your teacher says them. Then open your book and check your writing.

Give Me the Money!

UNIT 6

1 PRE-READING

Look at the pictures. Listen to your teacher tell the story.

22

Looking for Love

John is 52 years old. He is not married. Every day he comes home from work and eats dinner alone. Then he watches TV alone. At 11 o'clock he goes to bed alone.

John is not happy. He has a good job and a nice house, but he doesn't have love. He wants a wife.

How can John find a wife? One day he has an idea.

John is a painter, and he drives a small truck. He paints these words on his truck:

**WANTED — A WIFE
ARE YOU 35–45 YEARS OLD?
DO YOU LIKE CHILDREN, PETS,
AND QUIET TIMES?**

**PLEASE WRITE ME.
MY ADDRESS IS 307 S. SIXTH ST.
I AM A HARDWORKING MAN.**

Hundreds of women write letters to John. He reads all the letters. He likes one letter very much.

The letter is from Bobbi. Bobbi is 33 years old, and she is divorced. She has two children and a dog.

John calls Bobbi, and they meet. One week later, John paints his truck white.

"I'm not looking for love now," John says with a smile.

One year later, John and Bobbi are married.

23

2 VOCABULARY

Write the correct word on the line.

| alone | calls | hardworking | meets | nice | pets |

1. John doesn't have a wife or children. Every day he eats dinner _____alone_____.

2. John's house has three bedrooms and two bathrooms. It has a big kitchen and a lot of windows. It's a _____ house.

3. John works every day from eight o'clock in the morning to six o'clock in the evening. He is a _____ man.

4. John reads Bobbi's letter. Then he picks up his phone and _____ her.

5. Bobbi has a dog. That is OK with John because he likes _____.

6. When John _____ Bobbi, he says, "Hi. I'm John," and she says, "Hi. I'm Bobbi."

3 COMPREHENSION

UNDERSTANDING PRONOUNS

Who is it? What is it? Write the letter of your answer on the line.

_b_ 1. *He* is a painter.   a. his truck
____ 2. *It* is 307 S. Sixth Street.   b. John
____ 3. John reads *them*.   c. John's address
____ 4. *She* has two children and a dog.   d. the letters
____ 5. John paints *it* white.   e. Bobbi

REMEMBERING DETAILS

Circle the correct answer.

1. John is (**52** / 31) years old.

2. He is (married / not married).

3. He has a good job and a nice house, but he doesn't have (love / money).

4. He is (happy / not happy).

5. He is a (repairman / painter), and he drives a small truck.

6. He paints these words on his truck: WANTED — A (WIFE / JOB).

7. (Hundreds / Thousands) of women write letters to John.

24 Unit 6

4 DISCUSSION

A How can people find a husband or wife? Which ideas are good ideas? Check (✓) *YES* or *NO*.

Is it a good idea?	YES	NO
1. Look on the Internet.	☐	☐
2. Tell your parents: Please find a husband (or wife) for me.	☐	☐
3. Tell your friends: Please find a husband (or wife) for me.	☐	☐
4. Go dancing.	☐	☐
5. Go to a church, temple, or mosque.	☐	☐
6. Look for a husband or wife at work or at school.	☐	☐

B Which ideas do your classmates like? How many of your classmates checked *YES* for:

1? _____   2? _____   3? _____   4? _____   5? _____   6? _____

C What are other good ways to find a husband or wife? Share your ideas with the class.

5 WRITING

Imagine this: You are not married. You are looking for a husband or wife. You have a small truck. What will you paint on your truck? Write the words on the lines.

WANTED — A _____

ARE YOU _____ – _____ YEARS OLD?

DO YOU LIKE _____, _____,

AND _____?

PLEASE WRITE ME.

MY ADDRESS IS _____.

I AM _____.

UNIT 7

1 PRE-READING

Look at the pictures. Listen to your teacher tell the story.

License, Please

A man is driving a big black car through the mountains in Norway. He is driving fast.

A police officer sees the black car and follows it.

The black car goes around a curve. Then it goes around another curve. How fast is the black car going? It is going ten kilometers over the speed limit. That is too fast for the curves.

The police officer turns on his red light and his siren. The black car slows down, pulls over to the side of the road, and stops. The police car pulls over and stops, too.

The police officer walks to the black car. "License, please," he says. The man in the black car shows the police officer his license.

"Oh!" the police officer says and smiles. "Well! Have a nice day, sir," he says. Then he walks back to his police car and drives away.

The police officer doesn't give the man a ticket. Why not? The man in the black car was driving too fast, wasn't he? Yes, he was. But he is the king of Norway.

2 VOCABULARY

Match the words and the pictures. Write your answer on the line.

| curve | follow | king | license | mountains | pull over |

1. _mountains_   2. _____   3. _____

4. _____   5. _____   6. _____

3 COMPREHENSION

REMEMBERING DETAILS

Complete the sentences. Write your answer on the line.

1. The man is driving a big white car, right?

   No, he is driving a big _black car_.

2. The man is driving through the mountains in Peru, right?

   No, he is driving through the mountains in _____.

3. He is driving slowly, right?

   No, he is driving _____.

4. The car is going five kilometers over the speed limit, right?

   No, it is going _____.

5. The man is the president of Norway, right?

   No, he is the _____.

28 Unit 7

MAKING CONNECTIONS

Complete the sentences. Write the letter of your answer on the line.

1. The police officer sees the black car and __d__
2. The black car pulls over and ____
3. The police officer walks to the black car and ____
4. The police officer looks at the man's license and ____
5. The police officer walks back to his car and ____

a. smiles.
b. drives away.
c. says, "License, please."
d. follows it.
e. stops.

4 DISCUSSION

These people are driving too fast. Do they get a ticket in your country? Tell the class.

1. the president of your country
2. someone in the president's family 
3. a tourist from another country 
4. a man with a lot of money in his hand 

5 WRITING

Why do drivers in your country get a ticket? Make a list on your own paper. Then share your list with the class. For example:

The driver is driving too fast.
The driver doesn't stop at a stop sign.

License, Please 29

UNIT 8

1 PRE-READING

Look at the pictures. Listen to your teacher tell the story.

Election Day

Herb Casey wants to be mayor of his city. So he works hard. He puts up signs. "VOTE FOR HERB CASEY" the signs say. He knocks on doors and talks to people. "Please vote for me," he says. He mails letters to thousands of people. "Please vote for me," he writes. He gives speeches. "Vote for me!" he says in his speeches.

Finally, it is Election Day. It is time for people to vote. Herb works extra hard on Election Day. He puts up more signs and knocks on more doors. He calls people on the phone, too. "Today is Election Day," he says. "Please vote for me."

At eight o'clock in the evening, Herb stops making phone calls and goes to vote. It is ten minutes after eight when Herb arrives to vote. He is too late. Voting stops at eight o'clock. Herb cannot vote.

The next day, people count the votes. Is Herb Casey the new mayor? Does he win the election? No, he doesn't. He loses the election by one vote.

2 VOCABULARY

Match the words and the pictures. Write your answer on the line.

| call people on the phone | knock on doors | put up signs |
| give speeches | mail letters | vote |

1. _put up signs_    2.  _____   3. _____

4.  _____   5.  _____   6. _____

3 COMPREHENSION

UNDERSTANDING THE MAIN IDEAS

Complete the sentences. Circle the letter of the answer.

1. Herb works hard because
    a. he wants to be president of his country.
    b. he wants to be mayor of his city.
    c. he wants to be rich.

2. Herb loses the election because
    a. he doesn't put up signs.
    b. people don't like him.
    c. he doesn't vote.

3. Herb doesn't vote because
    a. he knows he will win the election.
    b. he arrives too late to vote.
    c. he is not in his city on election day.

REMEMBERING DETAILS

Herb works hard because he wants to be mayor of his city. What does he do? Check (✓) five answers.

- [✓] 1. He gives speeches.
- [ ] 2. He gives people money.
- [ ] 3. He puts up signs.
- [ ] 4. He calls people on the phone.
- [ ] 5. He mails letters.
- [ ] 6. He puts his picture in the newspaper.
- [ ] 7. He knocks on doors and talks to people.
- [ ] 8. He votes many times.

4 DISCUSSION / WRITING

A Complete the sentence below. Check (✓) *YES* or *NO*.

In my country, people who want to win an election…

	YES	NO
1. put up signs.	☐	☐
2. mail letters.	☐	☐
3. knock on doors.	☐	☐
4. give speeches.	☐	☐
5. call people on the phone.	☐	☐

6. _____
(other)

B Share your answers with the class.

C Think about people who want to win an election in your country. What do they do? What don't they do? On your own paper, make five sentences with the information from your discussion. For example:

They put up signs.
They don't mail letters.

Election Day

UNIT 9

1 PRE-READING

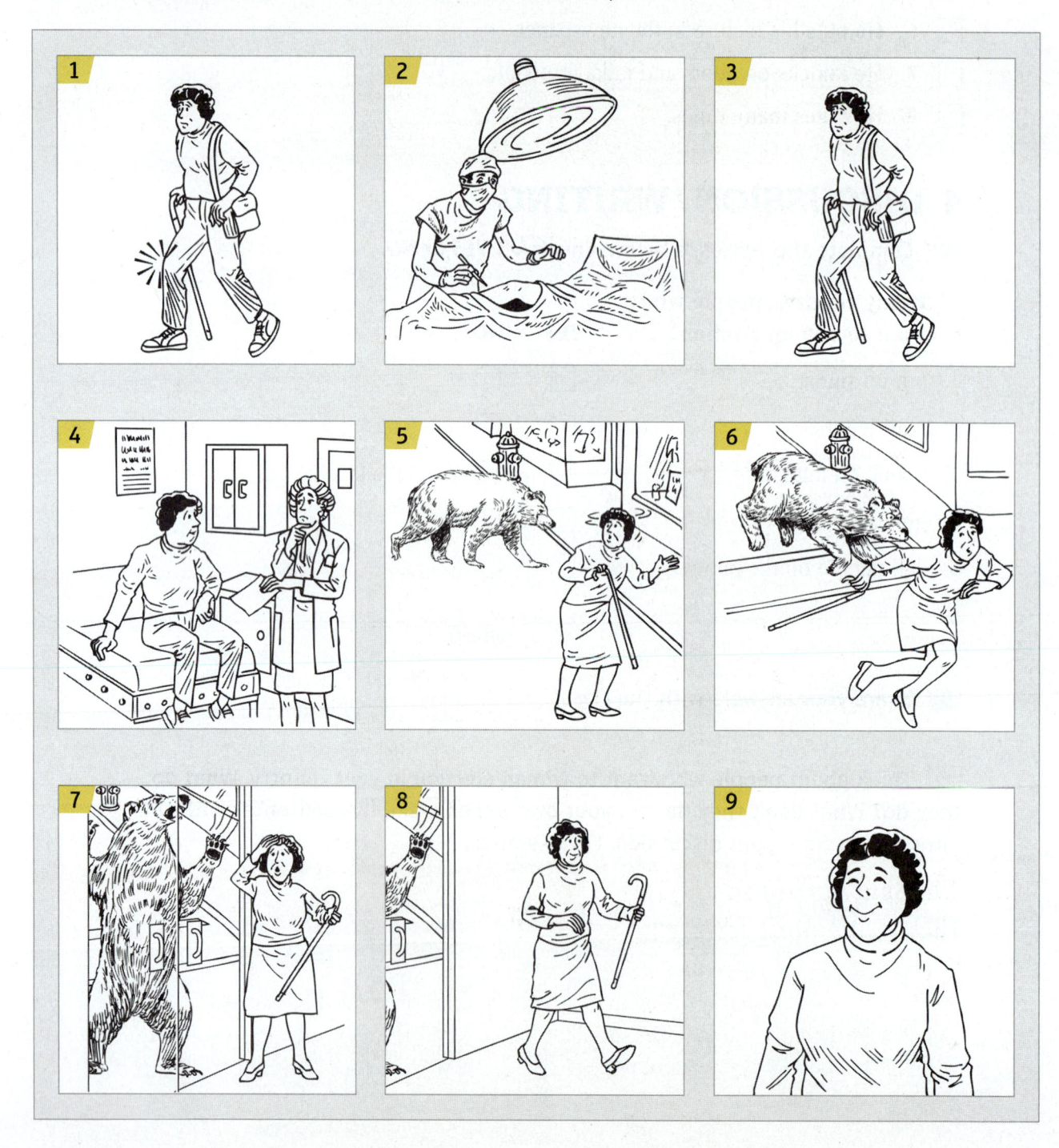

Look at the pictures. Listen to your teacher tell the story.

The Best Doctor

Connie is having trouble with her knee. Her knee hurts, and she walks with a limp. Her doctor tells her, "You need surgery on your knee." So Connie has surgery.

After the surgery, Connie's knee feels better. It doesn't hurt. But she still walks with a limp. Connie goes to many doctors. "Please help me," Connie says. "I don't want to walk with a limp." But the doctors can't help Connie. She still walks with a limp.

One morning, when Connie is walking to work, she sees something big and brown. What is it? Is it an animal? Yes, it is! It is a bear, and it is running toward Connie.

Connie lives in Alaska. In Alaska, bears come into the city sometimes. The bears are dangerous. They can kill people.

Connie runs toward a building, and the bear runs after her. The bear runs fast, and Connie runs fast, too; she doesn't think about her knee. Connie runs into the building and closes the door. The bear stands outside and growls.

Connie walks away from the door. She does not walk with a limp.

Connie never walks with a limp again, and she never has another problem with her knee. Connie went to many doctors, but the bear was the best doctor!

2 VOCABULARY

Write the correct word on the line.

| dangerous | hurts | limp | surgery | toward | trouble |

1. Connie has a problem: She is having _____trouble_____ with her knee.
2. "Ow!" Connie says when she walks. Her knee _____.
3. Connie can't walk fast because she walks with a _____.
4. Connie goes to a hospital and has _____ on her knee.
5. Connie can see the bear's face because it is running in her direction. It is running _____ Connie.
6. Bears sometimes kill people. They are _____.

3 COMPREHENSION

MAKING CONNECTIONS

Complete the sentences. Write the letter of your answer on the line.

1. Connie is having trouble _e_
2. She walks ____
3. Connie lives ____
4. Sometimes bears come ____
5. The bear runs ____
6. Connie runs ____

a. into a building.
b. into the city.
c. in Alaska.
d. toward Connie.
e. with her knee.
f. with a limp.

REVIEWING THE STORY

Write the correct word on the line.

Connie's knee hurts and she _____walks_____ with a limp, so she has
                                       1.
surgery. After the surgery, Connie's knee doesn't hurt, but she

_____ walks with a limp.
       2.
One day Connie is walking to _____ when a
                                    3.
_____ runs after her. Connie runs fast. She runs into a
       4.
_____. Connie never limps again, and she never has another
       5.
problem with her _____.
                          6.

36 Unit 9

4 DISCUSSION / WRITING

Connie goes to many doctors for help with her knee problem.

A Talk about going to the doctor in the United States. Answer the questions below. In a small group, take a guess. Write your group's answer on the line.

1. How many times a year do people in the United States go to the doctor?

   _____ times a year

2. When people go to a doctor in the United States, how many minutes are they with the doctor?

   _____ minutes

3. How much does it cost to see a doctor in the United States?

   $_____

4. When people go to the emergency room at a hospital in the United States, how much does it cost?

   $_____

B Share your group's answers with the class. (The correct answers are on page 83.)

C Write about going to the doctor. Answer the questions with complete sentences.

1. How many times a year do you go to the doctor?

   _____

   _____

2. How many minutes are you with the doctor?

   _____

   _____

3. How much does it cost to see a doctor in your country?

   _____

   _____

4. How much does it cost to go to the emergency room at a hospital in your country?

   _____

   _____

UNIT 10

1 PRE-READING

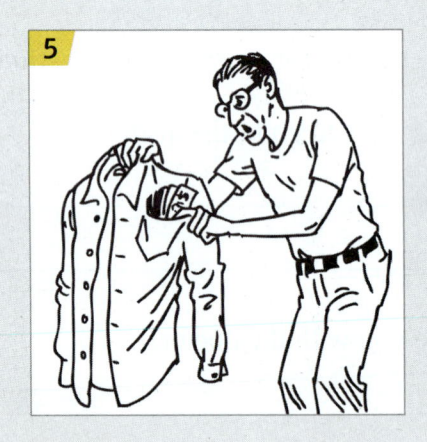

Look at the pictures. Listen to your teacher tell the story.

38

Larry's Favorite Shirt

Larry Hoffman likes to shop for clothes at thrift stores. There are no new clothes at thrift stores. There are only used clothes. But sometimes Larry finds nice clothes there.

One day Larry is shopping at a thrift store when he sees a blue shirt. Blue is Larry's favorite color. The shirt is size large—Larry's size. The price is $3.98. That's cheap! Larry buys the shirt.

At home, Larry tries on the shirt. It fits, and it looks good. When Larry takes the shirt off, he feels something in the pocket. What is it? Larry looks in the pocket. There is money in the pocket—a lot of money. Larry takes the money out of the pocket and counts it. Two thousand dollars! He holds the money in his hand and thinks for a minute or two. Then he takes the money and the shirt back to the thrift store.

Who gave the shirt to the thrift store? The people at the thrift store don't know. They give the money to the police. "We'll try to find the last owner of the shirt," the police tell Larry. "If we don't find the owner in 90 days, you can keep the money."

Ninety days later, Larry gets a phone call from the police. "We can't find the last owner of the shirt," a police officer tells him. "You can keep the money."

Larry is *very* happy with his blue shirt!

2 VOCABULARY

Write the correct word on the line.

| cheap | counts | fits | owner | used |

1. The clothes at a thrift store are not new. They are _____used_____.

2. The shirt is only $3.98. That is _____.

3. The shirt is not too big and not too small. It _____.

4. How much money is in the pocket? Larry wants to know, so he takes out the money and _____ it.

5. The police try to find the last _____ of the shirt.

3 COMPREHENSION

UNDERSTANDING THE MAIN IDEAS

Circle the correct word.

1. Larry Hoffman likes to shop for (books /(clothes)) at thrift stores.

2. He sees a (shirt / sweater) in size (large / medium).

3. He finds (money / candy) in the shirt pocket.

4. The police tell Larry, "If we don't find the owner in 90 (hours / days), you can keep the money.

5. The police (can / can't) find the owner of the money.

6. Larry can (keep / return) the money.

FINDING MORE INFORMATION

Read each sentence on the left. Which sentence on the right gives you more information? Write the letter of your answer on the line.

_b_ 1. Larry likes to shop at thrift stores.   a. It is money.

____ 2. The shirt is blue.   b. Sometimes he finds nice clothes there.

____ 3. Larry feels something in the pocket.   c. The people at the thrift store don't know.

____ 4. Who gave the shirt to the thrift store? d. That is Larry's favorite color.

____ 5. Larry gets a phone call from the police. e. "You can keep the money," a police officer tells him.

4 DISCUSSION

Larry likes to shop for clothes at thrift stores.

Where do you like to shop for clothes? Complete the sentence. Then share your writing in a small group.

I like to shop for clothes _____

because _____

_____ .

5 WRITING

A Prepare for a dictation. Practice with the sentences below. Follow the directions on page 83.

1. Try on a shirt.
2. Look in the pocket.
3. Take money out of the pocket.
4. Count the money.
5. Look happy.

B Cover the sentences above with a piece of paper. On the lines below, write the sentences as your teacher says them.

1. _____
2. _____
3. _____
4. _____
5. _____

C Uncover the sentences and check your writing.

UNIT 11

1 PRE-READING

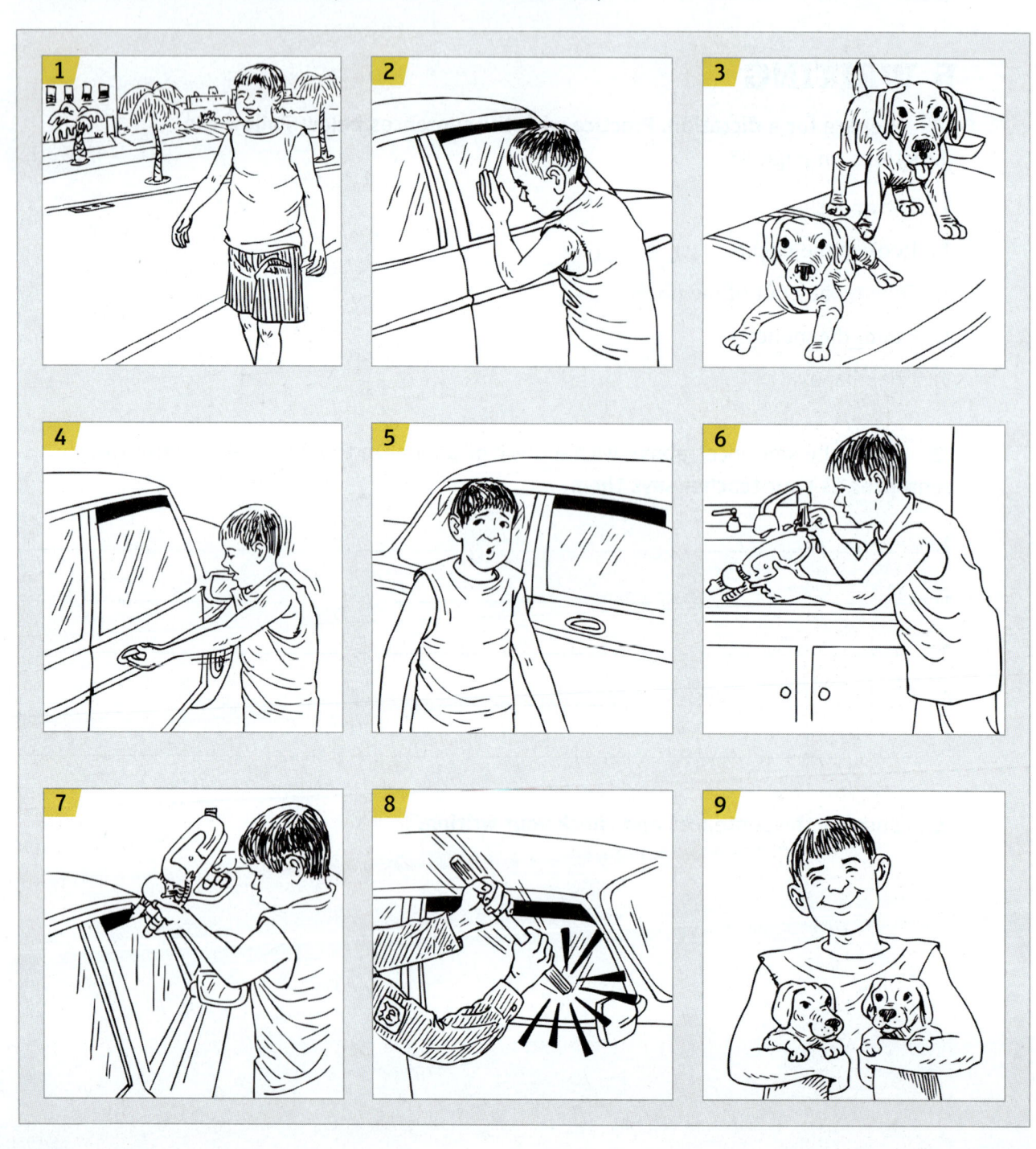

Look at the pictures. Listen to your teacher tell the story.

What a Boy! What a Toy!

Daniel Ayala, ten years old, is walking down the street on a hot summer day. It is 92 degrees (33.3 degrees Celsius). Daniel passes a parked car. He hears dogs barking, and he looks inside the car. Two puppies are in the car. The puppies look hot and thirsty. Daniel is worried about the puppies. "Maybe the puppies will die," he thinks.

Daniel tries to open the car doors, but they are locked. Daniel looks around. There are no people on the street. Nobody can help him.

Daniel runs home and gets his toy water gun. It is a big one—it holds a lot of water. Daniel fills his water gun with cool water. Then he runs back to the car.

The car windows are open a little. Daniel squirts water at the puppies. He squirts water on their faces and into their mouths. For one hour, Daniel stands next to the car. Every five minutes, he squirts water at the puppies.

Finally, help comes. A police officer breaks a car window and opens a door. Daniel picks up the puppies. Thanks to Daniel, they are OK.

2 VOCABULARY

Write the correct word on the line.

| cool | degrees | fills | locked | puppies | worried |

1. It is very hot. The temperature is 92 ___degrees___.

2. The two dogs in the car are young. They are _____.

3. Daniel thinks, "Maybe the puppies will die." He is _____ about the puppies.

4. Daniel can't open the car doors. They are _____.

5. Daniel puts water in his toy gun. He _____ it with water.

6. The water is cold, but not very cold. It is _____.

3 COMPREHENSION

REMEMBERING DETAILS

Complete the sentences. Write your answer on the line.

1. Daniel is eight years old, right?

    No, he is _ten years old_____.

2. It is a cold winter day, right?

    No, it is a _____.

3. Three puppies are in the car, right?

    No, _____.

4. The puppies look hungry, right?

    No, they look _____.

5. Daniel stands next to the car for 20 minutes, right?

    No, he stands next to the car for _____.

6. A paramedic breaks a car window, right?

    No, a _____.

44   Unit 11

UNDERSTANDING PRONOUNS

Who is it? What is it? Write the letter of your answer on the line.

_d_ 1. *He* squirts water at the puppies.   a. his water gun

____ 2. *They* look hot and thirsty.   b. the car windows

____ 3. *They* are locked.   c. the car doors

____ 4. Daniel fills *it* with cool water.   d. Daniel

____ 5. *They* are open a little.   e. the puppies

4 DISCUSSION

A Imagine this: You are walking down the street on a hot summer day. You see two puppies in a locked car. The puppies look hot and thirsty. You do not have a water gun. What do you do? Check (✓) your answer.

☐ call the police

☐ break a car window

☐ look for the puppies' owner

☐ do nothing

B Explain your answer in a small group.

5 WRITING

A Prepare for a dictation. Practice with the sentences below. Follow the directions on page 83.

1. Walk down the street.
2. Look inside the car.
3. Try to open the car doors.
4. Look around.
5. Run home.
6. Fill your water gun with water.
7. Run back to the car.

B Now close your book. On your own paper, write the sentences as your teacher reads them. Then open your book and check your writing.

What a Boy! What a Toy! 45

UNIT 12

1 PRE-READING

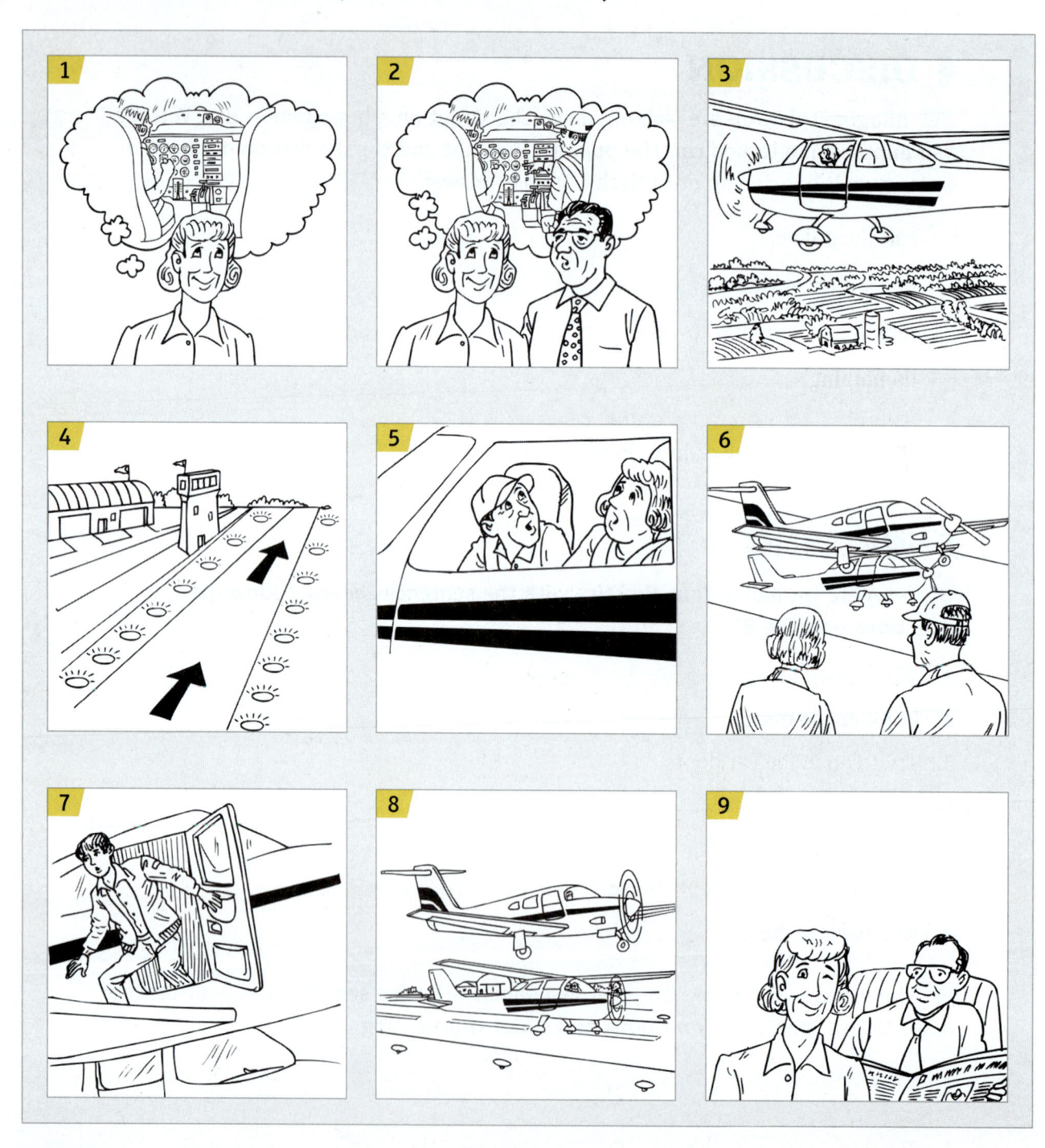

Look at the pictures. Listen to your teacher tell the story.

The Flying Lesson

The two planes after landing

Barbara wants to be a pilot. She wants to fly a small airplane. "I want to take flying lessons," she tells her husband.

"Flying lessons?" her husband says. "Flying is dangerous!"

"Don't worry," Barbara says. "I'll be fine."

Barbara takes flying lessons. Today she is practicing landing. She is in a small airplane with her teacher. Barbara sees the airport. Then she sees the runway. She flies lower and lower. "Good!" her teacher says.

Barbara hears a loud noise on the top of the airplane. "What's that?" Barbara asks her teacher.

"I don't know!" the teacher says. "Land the plane, Barbara. Land the plane."

Barbara lands the airplane. She and her teacher get out of the airplane. They see another, bigger airplane. It is on top of their airplane.

The pilot gets out of the bigger airplane. "Sorry," the pilot says. "I was landing, too. I didn't see you."

Later Barbara goes home. "How was your flying lesson?" her husband asks.

"Fine," Barbara says. "Today I landed two airplanes—a small airplane and a bigger airplane."

"No problems?" her husband asks.

Barbara smiles. "No," she says. "No problems."

47

2 VOCABULARY

Write the correct word on the line.

| dangerous | landing | lessons | noise | on top of | practicing |

1. Barbara tells her husband, "I want to be a pilot." Her husband is worried. "Flying is ____dangerous____!" he says.

2. Barbara wants to learn to fly an airplane. So, she pays a teacher $40 an hour to teach her. She takes flying _____.

3. Barbara flies lower and lower because she is _____ the airplane.

4. Barbara lands the airplane. Then she lands it again and again. She is _____ landing.

5. Barbara hears something. "What was that _____?" she asks her teacher.

6. The loud noise is not under the airplane. It is _____ the airplane.

3 COMPREHENSION

REMEMBERING DETAILS

Complete the sentences. Write your answer on the line.

1. Barbara wants to be a mechanic, right?

   No, she wants to be a _pilot_____.

2. She wants to fly a big airplane, right?

   No, she wants to fly a _____.

3. The bigger airplane is under the small airplane, right?

   No, it is _____.

4. The pilot gets out of the bigger plane and says, "Hello," right?

   No, the pilot says, "_____"

5. Barbara tells her husband, "Today I landed three airplanes," right?

   No, she tells him, "Today I landed _____"

48   Unit 12

WHO SAYS IT?

Write the letter of your answer on the line.

_d_ 1. "How was your flying lesson?"   a. Barbara

____ 2. "Land the plane, Barbara."   b. the teacher

____ 3. "I want to take flying lessons."   c. the pilot of the bigger airplane

____ 4. "Sorry. I was landing, too. I didn't see you."   d. Barbara's husband

4 DISCUSSION

Barbara wants to fly a small airplane. And you? What do you want to do?

A Draw a picture on your own paper. In the picture, you are doing what you want to do. Look at the example on the right.

B Show your picture to a small group of classmates. Tell your classmates what you want to do.

5 WRITING

A Tell your teacher what you want to do. Your teacher will make a list on the board. For example:

Kenji   sleep

B Use the information on the board to write five sentences. For example:

Kenji wants to sleep.

1. _____
2. _____
3. _____
4. _____
5. _____

The Flying Lesson   49

UNIT 13

1 PRE-READING

Look at the pictures. Listen to your teacher tell the story.

Two Happy Men

Pedro Rossi is happy—he is very, very happy! He won the lottery! He won $500,000!

Pedro is happy for a few minutes. Then he remembers: his lottery ticket! He threw it in the garbage can!

Pedro runs to the garbage can and looks inside. The garbage can is empty!

"Where is the garbage?" Pedro asks his wife.

"The garbage is gone," his wife says. "The garbage truck came this morning." The garbage truck takes the garbage to the garbage dump. Pedro goes to the dump. He looks in the garbage for two days. He doesn't find his lottery ticket.

Pedro lives in a town in Brazil. Pedro tells the people in the town, "Look for my lottery ticket at the dump. If you find it, I will give you half the money."

Every day hundreds of people go to the dump. They look in the garbage for the ticket. Five days later, a man finds it. Pedro gives the man $250,000.

Pedro won $500,000 in the lottery. Now he has only $250,000. But he is not sad. "Before, one man was happy," Pedro says. "Now two men are happy!"

2 VOCABULARY

Match the words and the pictures. Write your answer on the line.

| dump | garbage can | garbage truck | half | lottery ticket | town |

1. _____half_____  2.  _____ 3. _____

4.  _____ 5.  _____ 6. _____

3 COMPREHENSION

REMEMBERING DETAILS

Which sentence is correct? Circle *a* or *b*.

1. a. Pedro won $5,000 in the lottery.
   b. Pedro won $500,000 in the lottery.

2. a. Pedro threw his lottery ticket in the garbage can.
   b. Pedro threw his money in the garbage can.

3. a. Pedro lives in a city in Mexico.
   b. Pedro lives in a town in Brazil.

4. a. Pedro tells people, "If you find the lottery ticket, I will give you $1,000."
   b. Pedro tells people, "If you find the lottery ticket, I will give you half the money."

5. a. A man finds Pedro's ticket at the garbage dump.
   b. Pedro finds his ticket at the garbage dump.

52   Unit 13

LEARNING PAST TENSE FORMS

What is the past tense of the verb? Draw a line to it.

1. is   came
2. win   was
3. throw   won
4. come   threw

4 DISCUSSION

Pedro and the people in his town looked for his $500,000 lottery ticket at the garbage dump.

A Imagine this: There is a lottery ticket at the garbage dump in your city. Will you look in the garbage for the ticket? Check (✓) YES or NO.

Will you look for it?	YES	NO
1. The lottery ticket is for $100.	☐	☐
2. The lottery ticket is for $1,000.	☐	☐
3. The lottery ticket is for $100,000.	☐	☐
4. The lottery ticket is for $1,000,000.	☐	☐

B Count your classmates. How many people will look in the garbage for:

$100? _____ $1,000? _____ $100,000? _____ $1,000,000? _____

5 WRITING

Imagine this: You won $500,000 in the lottery! What will you do with the money? Write three sentences. Then share your writing in a small group. For example:

I will buy a house.
I will go to Hawaii.
I will save the money for my children's education.

1. _____
2. _____
3. _____

UNIT 14

1 PRE-READING

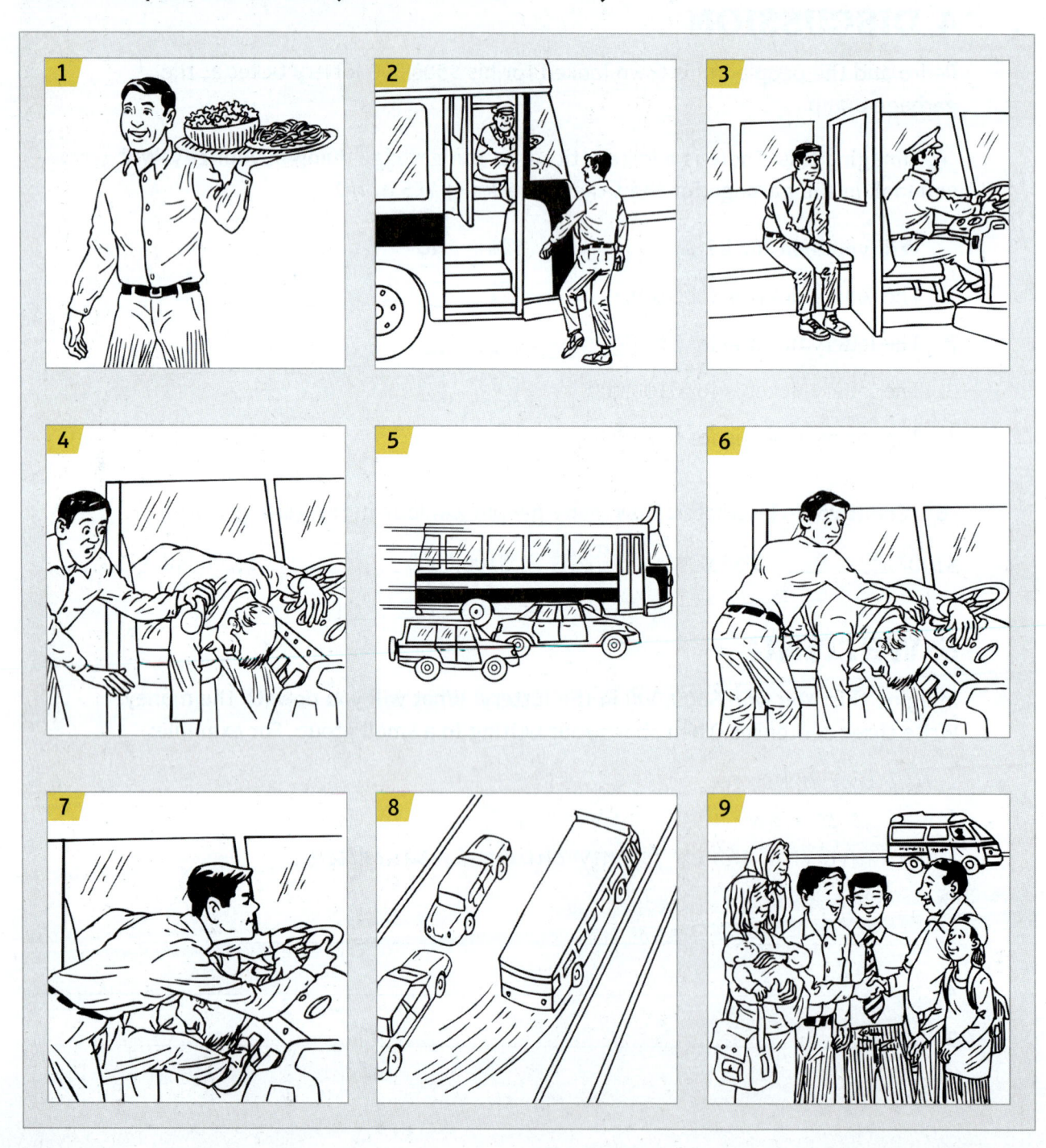

Look at the pictures. Listen to your teacher tell the story.

54

Speed

Ramya de Silva and bus

Ramya is a waiter. He works at a restaurant from eight o'clock in the morning to four o'clock in the afternoon.

One day at four o'clock, Ramya leaves work and gets on a bus to go home. He sits down behind the bus driver.

Suddenly the bus driver leans forward. His head is almost to the floor. Ramya jumps up. "Are you OK, sir?" he asks the bus driver. The bus driver doesn't answer.

The bus is going fast now, and nobody is driving it. Ramya pulls on the bus driver. He tries to pull him out of the driver's seat. But the bus driver is a big man. Ramya can't move him.

Now the bus is going really fast. Ramya has to stop the bus! He puts his hands on the steering wheel. He puts his left foot on the brake. He drives the bus to the right side of the street. Slowly he stops the bus.

An ambulance arrives and takes the bus driver to the hospital. All the passengers on the bus are OK.

Ramya works at a restaurant. He is a waiter. But one day for ten minutes, Ramya was a bus driver—a bus driver and a hero.

2 VOCABULARY

Write the correct word on the line.

| behind | brake | hero | passengers | steering wheel | waiter |

1. Ramya works at a restaurant. He brings people their food. He is a _____waiter_____.

2. Ramya doesn't like to sit in the back of the bus. He likes to sit in the front of the bus, in the seat _____ the bus driver.

3. Ramya wants to drive the bus to the side of the street, so he puts his hands on the _____.

4. Ramya wants to stop the bus, so he puts his foot on the _____.

5. How are the people on the bus? The _____ are all OK.

6. Ramya is not a bus driver, and he is not a big man, but he drives the bus and stops it. The passengers say, "Thank you, Ramya! Thank you!" Ramya is a _____.

3 COMPREHENSION

REMEMBERING DETAILS

Which sentence is correct? Circle *a* or *b*.

1. a. Ramya gets on a train to go home.
   (b.) Ramya gets on a bus to go home.

2. a. The bus driver leans backward.
   b. The bus driver leans forward.

3. a. The bus driver's head is on the floor.
   b. The bus driver's head is almost to the floor.

4. a. Ramya tries to push the bus driver out of the driver's seat.
   b. Ramya tries to pull the bus driver out of the driver's seat.

5. a. The bus driver is a small man.
   b. The bus driver is a big man.

6. a. Ramya can't move him.
   b. Ramya can move him.

UNDERSTANDING PRONOUNS

Who is it? What is it? Write the letter of your answer on the line.

_c_ 1. *He* is a waiter. a. the steering wheel

____ 2. Ramya can't move *him*. b. the brake

____ 3. Ramya puts his hands on *it*. c. Ramya

____ 4. Ramya puts his left foot on *it*. d. the passengers

____ 5. *It* takes the bus driver to the hospital. e. the bus driver

____ 6. *They* are all OK. f. the ambulance

4 DISCUSSION / WRITING

Ramya takes the bus home. How do the people in your class get home?

A Walk around the room. Ask five people the question below. Write each person's name on a line. Then check (✓) each person's answer.

How do you get home?

Name	take the bus	take the subway	drive	walk	go by bike	ride with someone	other
1. _____	☐	☐	☐	☐	☐	☐	☐
2. _____	☐	☐	☐	☐	☐	☐	☐
3. _____	☐	☐	☐	☐	☐	☐	☐
4. _____	☐	☐	☐	☐	☐	☐	☐
5. _____	☐	☐	☐	☐	☐	☐	☐

B Write five sentences with the information above. For example:

Kanjana drives home.
Alfredo gets a ride with Francisco.

1. _____
2. _____
3. _____
4. _____
5. _____

Speed

UNIT 15

1 PRE-READING

Look at the pictures. Listen to your teacher tell the story.

The Kind Waitress

Every evening at six o'clock, an old man goes to a restaurant near his house. He eats dinner. After dinner, he drinks coffee and talks to the people at the restaurant.

The old man's name is Bill. Bill eats at the restaurant every evening because he is lonely. His wife died, and he has no children.

Every evening the same waitress brings Bill his dinner. After dinner, she pours his coffee. The waitress's name is Cara. She is 17 years old.

Cara is kind to Bill. She knows he is lonely, so she talks to him. If Bill is late for dinner, she calls him. "Are you OK?" she asks him.

One evening Bill doesn't come to the restaurant. Cara calls him, but he doesn't answer the phone. Cara calls the police. "Please go to Bill's house," Cara tells the police.

Later, the police call Cara at the restaurant. "Bill died in his sleep," the police tell her. Bill was 82 years old.

A week later, a man comes to the restaurant. "I have something for Cara," the man says. The man gives Cara a check for $500,000. The money is from Bill.

"This money is for me? From Bill?" Cara asks the man.

"Yes," the man answers.

"But…why?" Cara asks the man.

"Bill liked you," the man says. "You were kind to him."

2 VOCABULARY

Write the correct word on the line.

| calls | check | kind | late | lonely | waitress |

1. Bill usually goes to the restaurant at 6:00. One day he arrives at 6:20. Bill is _____late_____.

2. Bill has no family, and he lives alone. He is _____.

3. Cara works at the restaurant. She brings Bill his food. She is a _____.

4. Cara knows that Bill is lonely, so she talks to him. She is _____ to Bill.

5. Cara knows Bill's phone number. If he is late for dinner, Cara _____ him.

6. The man gives Bill's money to Cara. It is a _____ for $500,000.

3 COMPREHENSION

UNDERSTANDING THE MAIN IDEAS

Circle the letter of the best answer.

1. Bill goes to the restaurant because
    a. the food is very good.
    b. he doesn't like to cook.
    c. he is lonely.

2. Cara talks to Bill because
    a. she knows Bill is rich.
    b. she likes to talk to people.
    c. she knows Bill is lonely.

3. Bill gives his money to Cara because
    a. she was kind to him.
    b. she needs the money very much.
    c. she is his daughter.

REMEMBERING DETAILS

Which sentence is correct? Circle *a* or *b*.

1. a. Every morning an old man eats breakfast at a restaurant near his house.
   b. (circled) Every evening an old man eats dinner at a restaurant near his house.

2. a. After dinner, Bill drinks tea and reads the newspaper.
   b. After dinner, Bill drinks coffee and talks to the people at the restaurant.

3. a. Bill has no children.
   b. Bill has three children.

4. a. Cara is 17 years old.
   b. Cara is 37 years old.

5. a. Cara tells the police, "Please take Bill to the hospital."
   b. Cara tells the police, "Please go to Bill's house."

6. a. When Bill dies, he gives Cara $500.
   b. When Bill dies, he gives Cara $500,000.

4 DISCUSSION / WRITING

Bill was lonely, so he went to the restaurant every evening.

A What can people do when they're lonely? Go dancing? Call a friend? Share your ideas with the class. Your teacher will write your ideas on the board.

B What about you? What do you do when you're lonely? Find three ways to complete the sentence.

When I'm lonely, I . . .

_____

_____

_____

C Share your writing in a small group.

The Kind Waitress

UNIT 16

1 PRE-READING

Look at the pictures. Listen to your teacher tell the story.

Grandfather Hada's Favorite Soup

It is New Year's Day in Japan. The Hada family is eating a special New Year's soup. The soup has chicken, vegetables, and mochi in it. Mochi are rice cakes.

Grandfather Hada likes mochi. He takes a big bite of mochi. Then he begins to cough.

Grandfather Hada coughs and coughs. He can't stop coughing. The mochi is stuck in his throat.

Grandfather Hada's face is purple. He can't breathe. Someone runs to the phone and calls an ambulance. When will the ambulance arrive? Maybe in five or ten minutes. That will be too late.

Grandfather Hada's daughter gets the vacuum cleaner. She turns the vacuum cleaner on and turns the power to "high." She puts the vacuum cleaner hose into Grandfather Hada's throat. Whoosh! The mochi comes out of his throat and goes into the vacuum cleaner. Now Grandfather Hada can breathe.

Nine minutes later, the ambulance arrives, and paramedics check Grandfather Hada. He is fine.

Next year, on New Year's Day, the Hada family will eat a special soup. The soup will have chicken and vegetables in it. But it will have no mochi!

2 VOCABULARY

Write the correct word on the line.

| bite | breathe | check | stuck | throat |

1. Grandfather Hada loves to eat mochi. So he doesn't put a little mochi into his mouth. He opens his mouth and takes a big _____*bite*_____.

2. The mochi goes into Grandfather's mouth. Then it goes down into his _____.

3. The mochi is in Grandfather Hada's throat. It doesn't go up, and it doesn't go down. It is _____.

4. Grandfather Hada's face is purple because no air is going into his body. He can't _____.

5. The paramedics examine Grandfather Hada. They listen to his heart, and they listen to his breathing. They _____ to see if he is OK.

3 COMPREHENSION

REMEMBERING DETAILS

One word in each sentence is not correct. Find the word and cross it out. Write the correct word.

1. It is New Year's Day in ~~China~~. *Japan*

2. The Hada family is eating a special New Year's cake.

3. The soup has fish, vegetables, and mochi in it.

4. Mochi are potato cakes.

5. Grandfather Hada loves to make mochi.

6. The mochi is stuck in Grandfather Hada's tooth.

7. Grandfather Hada's face is white.

8. Next year, the New Year's soup will have no vegetables in it.

MAKING CONNECTIONS

Complete the sentences. Write the letter of your answer on the line.

1. Grandfather Hada takes a big bite of mochi and __e__
2. Someone runs to the phone and ____
3. Grandfather Hada's daughter turns the vacuum cleaner on and ____
4. The mochi comes out of Grandfather Hada's throat and ____
5. Paramedics arrive and ____

a. turns the power to "high."
b. goes into the vacuum cleaner.
c. check Grandfather Hada.
d. calls an ambulance.
e. begins to cough.

4 DISCUSSION / WRITING

A Talk about your favorite foods. First, answer the questions. Write your answer on the line.

What do you like to eat? _____
(For example: *I like to eat pizza.*)

When do you like to eat it? _____
(For example: *I like to eat it late at night.*)

B Tell your teacher your answers. Your teacher will make a list on the board. For example:

Who	What	When
Aldo	pizza	late at night
Adriana	ice cream	in the summer

C Walk around the room. Tell your classmates about your favorite food and when you like to eat it.

D Make five sentences with the information on the board. For example:

Aldo likes to eat pizza, and he eats it late at night.
Adriana likes to eat ice cream, but she eats it only in the summer.

1. _____
2. _____
3. _____
4. _____
5. _____

UNIT 17

1 PRE-READING

Look at the pictures. Listen to your teacher tell the story.

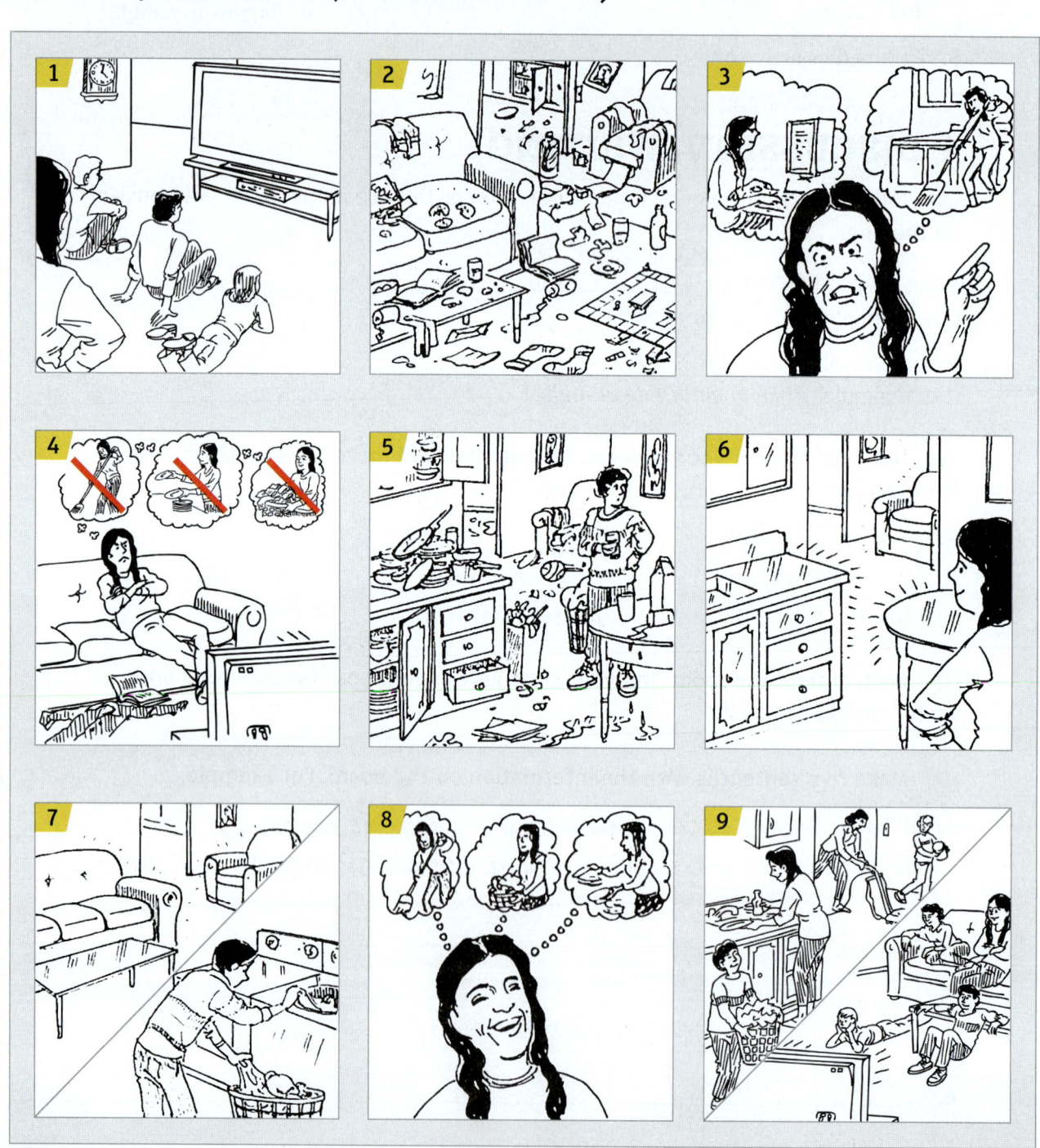

No More Housework!

It is five o'clock in the evening when Rene Wagner comes home from work. She walks into the living room and looks at her three children. The children are 14, 13, and 9 years old. They are watching TV.

The living room is a mess. There are empty glasses and dirty socks on the floor. There are cookies on the sofa. Games and toys are everywhere.

Rene is angry. "This place is a mess!" she tells her children. "I can't work all day and then do housework all evening. I'm not going to do housework!"

And so, Rene doesn't do housework. She doesn't clean. She doesn't wash dishes. She doesn't wash clothes. Every evening she sits on the sofa and watches TV.

After two weeks, every plate, fork, and glass in the house is dirty. All the children's clothes are dirty, too. Every garbage can is full. The house is a mess.

Then, one day Rene comes home from work and gets a big surprise. The kitchen is clean. The children cleaned the kitchen!

The next day, the living room is clean, and the children are washing their clothes.

Rene tells her children, "OK, I'll do housework again. But you have to help me."

Now, Rene and her three children do the housework together. Then they *all* sit on the sofa and watch TV!

2 VOCABULARY

Match the words and the pictures. Write the correct number on the line.

_8_ empty glasses
___ games
___ plate
___ dirty socks
___ toys
___ fork
___ cookies
___ sofa

3 COMPREHENSION

REMEMBERING DETAILS

Which sentence is correct? Circle *a* or *b*.

1. a. Rene has one child.
   b. Rene has three children.

2. a. When Rene comes home from work, her children are watching TV in the living room.
   b. When Rene comes home from work, her children are playing games in the kitchen.

3. a. Rene is angry. She says, "Turn off the TV!"
   b. Rene is angry. She says, "This place is a mess!"

4. a. Rene doesn't do housework for two months.
   b. Rene doesn't do housework for two weeks.

5. a. Rene gets a big surprise: Her children cleaned the kitchen!
   b. Rene gets a big surprise: Her friends cleaned the kitchen!

UNDERSTANDING PRONOUNS

Who is it? What is it? Write the letter of your answer on the line.

_b_ 1. *They* are 14, 13, and 9 years old.
____ 2. The children are watching *it*.
____ 3. *It* is a mess.
____ 4. *They* are everywhere.

a. games and toys
b. Rene's children
c. the living room
d. TV

4 DISCUSSION

What housework do you do? Check (✓) your answers. Then show your answers to a classmate. Are your answers and your classmate's answers the same?

	ALWAYS	SOMETIMES	NEVER
1. I wash the dishes.	☐	☐	☐
2. I clean.	☐	☐	☐
3. I wash the clothes.	☐	☐	☐
4. I make the beds.	☐	☐	☐
5. I cook.	☐	☐	☐
6. I empty the garbage cans.	☐	☐	☐

5 WRITING

What is Rene doing in picture 1? Write your answer on line 1. What is Rene doing in pictures 2, 3, and 4? Write your answers on the lines.

1. Rene is cleaning.
2. _____
3. _____
4. _____

UNIT 18

1 PRE-READING

Look at the pictures. Listen to your teacher tell the story.

70

The Bottle

Ake Viking is a young sailor. He is on a ship near Sweden. There is nothing to do on the ship, and Ake is bored. Ake writes this letter in English:

> *Are you a young woman?*
> *Do you want to marry a handsome young Swede?*
> *Please write me.*
>
> *Ake Viking*

Ake writes his address on the letter. Then he puts the letter in a bottle and throws the bottle into the sea.

Two years later, Sebastiano Puzzo is fishing near his home in Italy. He sees a bottle in the water. He takes the bottle out of the water and opens it. Inside the bottle, he finds Ake's letter.

Sebastiano takes the letter home to his daughter. Her name is Paolina, and she is 18 years old. Sebastiano and Paolina read the letter and laugh.

Just for fun, Paolina writes a letter to Ake. She sends him a photo, too.

Ake reads Paolina's letter and writes a letter to her. Then she writes a letter to him. For one year, Ake and Paolina write letters. Ake doesn't know Italian, and Paolina doesn't know Swedish, so they write in English.

In one letter, Ake writes:

Dear Paolina,
   I want to meet you. Is it OK if I visit you in Italy?

Ake

Paolina writes that it is OK, so Ake goes to Italy. He meets Paolina and her family. Two months later, Paolina marries the handsome young Swede.

2 VOCABULARY

Match the words and the pictures. Write your answer on the line.

| address | bottle | sailor | sea | ship | throw |

1. _____sailor_____   2. _____   3. _____

4. _____   5. _____   6. _____

3 COMPREHENSION

REMEMBERING DETAILS

Complete the sentences. Write your answer on the line.

1. Ake is on a ship near Spain, right?

   No, he is on a ship near _Sweden_____.

2. There is a lot to do on the ship, right?

   No, there is _____.

3. Paolina is 21 years old, right?

   No, she is _____.

4. Ake and Paolina write for three years, right?

   No, they write for _____.

5. They write their letters in Italian, right?

   No, they write in _____.

72   Unit 18

MAKING CONNECTIONS

Complete the sentences. Write the letter of your answer on the line.

1. Ake puts his letter in a bottle and __d__
2. Sebastiano Puzzo takes the bottle out of the water and _____
3. Sebastiano and Paolina read the letter and _____
4. Ake reads Paolina's letter and _____

a. laugh.
b. writes a letter to her.
c. brings it home to his daughter.
d. throws it into the sea.

4 DISCUSSION

Ake is from Sweden, and Paolina is from Italy. Ake doesn't speak Italian, and Paolina doesn't speak Swedish. When they talk, they speak English.

A Will Ake and Paolina be happy together? What do you think? Put an *X* somewhere on the line between *YES* and *NO*.

YES • **NO**

B Explain your answer in a small group.

5 WRITING

A Imagine this: You want to write a letter, put your letter in a bottle, and throw the bottle into the sea. What will you write? Make a list of possible sentences. Write the sentences on the board. For example:

If you find this letter, please write me.
You can write me in English or Chinese.
My address is: 303 Center Street, Whitewater, WI 53190, USA.
I am single.

B Now write your letter on the lines below.

_____
_____
_____
_____
_____

The Bottle

UNIT 19

1 PRE-READING

Look at the pictures. Listen to your teacher tell the story.

Whose Money Is It?

Louise Stamberg likes to save money. But she doesn't like banks. So she doesn't put her money in banks. She hides it in her house. She puts her money in cans. Then she puts the cans above the ceiling in her kitchen.

Louise writes "Olga" on some cans of money. Olga is Louise's niece. "This money is for Olga," Louise thinks. Louise doesn't tell Olga about the money. She doesn't tell anyone about the money.

When she is an old woman, Louise Stamberg dies. Then her niece Olga moves into Louise's house. Olga lives in the house for many years. Then she sells the house to Brian Williams.

Mr. Williams wants to remodel the kitchen. He hires a carpenter to do the work. The carpenter is fixing the ceiling when he finds 12 cans. He opens the cans, and what does he find? He finds money—a lot of money. He finds $150,000.

"It's my money!" the carpenter says. "I found it!"

"No, it's not your money," Mr. Williams says. "This is my house, so it's my money."

When Olga learns about the money, she says, "No, it's not your money. The name 'Olga' is on some of the cans."

A judge must decide: Whose money is it? Is it the carpenter's money? Is it Mr. Williams' money? Or is it Olga's money? What does the judge decide? What do you think?

2 VOCABULARY

Write the correct word on the line.

| ceiling | found | hides | hires | judge | remodel |

1. Louise Stamberg doesn't want people to find her money. So, she _____*hides*_____ it.

2. When Olga sits in her kitchen and looks up, she doesn't see the cans of money. She sees only the _____.

3. The kitchen in Mr. Williams' house is old. He wants to paint the kitchen, fix the ceiling, and buy a new refrigerator. He wants to _____ the kitchen.

4. Mr. Williams asks a carpenter, "Can you remodel my kitchen? I'll pay you $20 an hour to do the work." The carpenter says, "Yes, I'll do the work." Mr. Williams _____ the carpenter.

5. The carpenter finds the money above the ceiling. Later he says, "It is my money because I _____ it."

6. Whose money is it? Olga, Mr. Williams, and the carpenter go to court. They want a _____ to decide.

3 COMPREHENSION

UNDERSTANDING THE MAIN IDEAS

Answer the questions. Circle *a* or *b*.

1. Why does Louise Stamberg hide money in her house?
   a. She is sick and can't go to the bank.
   (b.) She doesn't like banks.

2. Where does Louise hide the money?
   a. She hides it above the ceiling in her kitchen.
   b. She hides it under the floor in her kitchen.

3. What does Louise write on some cans of money?
   a. She writes the name "Olga."
   b. She writes, "Do not open."

4. Who is Olga?
   a. She is Louise Stamberg's sister.
   b. She is Louise Stamberg's niece.

5. How does the carpenter find the money?
   a. He finds it when he is fixing the ceiling.
   b. He finds it when he is putting new lights in the kitchen.

WHO SAYS IT?

Who says it? Write the letter of your answer on the line.

_d_ 1. "I found it, so it's my money."   a. Olga

____ 2. "This money is for Olga."   b. Louise Stamberg

____ 3. "This is my house, so it's my money."   c. Mr. Williams

____ 4. "My name is on some of the cans, so it's my money."   d. the carpenter

4 DISCUSSION

A Imagine this: You are the judge in the story. Whose money is it? What do you decide? Check (✓) your answer.

☐ All the money is for Olga.

☐ All the money is for Mr. Williams.

☐ All the money is for the carpenter.

☐ Some of the money is for _____, and some of the money is for _____.

B Explain your answer in a small group. Can you guess the real judge's decision? The answer is on page 83.

5 WRITING

A Prepare for a dictation. Practice with the sentences below. Follow the directions on page 83.

1. Put the money in cans.
2. Write "Olga" on the cans.
3. Put the cans above the ceiling.
4. Fix the ceiling.
5. Open the cans.

B Now close your book. On your own paper, write the sentences as your teacher says them. Then open your book and check your writing.

UNIT 20

1 PRE-READING

Look at the pictures. Listen to your teacher tell the story.

78

The Gold Ring

It is 1942. David Cox is a soldier in the U.S. Army. David is in a camp in Germany. He is a prisoner of war. There is almost no food in the camp, and David is very hungry.

A soldier from Russia is in the camp, too. The Russian soldier has some chocolate bars.

David has a gold ring. It is a special ring—a gift from his parents. David takes off the ring and gives it to the Russian soldier. The Russian soldier gives David two chocolate bars.

David survives the war. He goes back to the United States, gets married, and has three children.

The Russian soldier survives the war, too. He goes back to Russia. On his way home, he goes through Hungary.

The Russian soldier has almost no food. But he has the gold ring. He gives the ring to a Hungarian woman. The Hungarian woman gives him food.

Many years later, the Hungarian woman gives the ring to her grandson. His name is Martin. Martin likes the ring very much. He wears it every day. One day Martin looks inside the ring. He sees writing. It says:

David C. Cox
Greensboro, NC. 10/4/18

Who is David C. Cox? Martin wants to know. He looks on the Internet. He finds a David C. Cox in Greensboro, North Carolina. He was born on October 4, 1918. He died in 1994.

But there is another David C. Cox in North Carolina—David C. Cox, Jr. He is the soldier's son. In 2012, Martin sends the gold ring to the soldier's son. It is a gift from Martin.

After 70 years, the gold ring is home.

2 VOCABULARY

Write the correct word on the line.

| gift | prisoner | soldier | survive | writing |

1. David Cox is in the U.S. Army. He is a _____soldier_____.

2. David is in a camp in Germany. He is a _____.

3. David and the Russian soldier don't die in World War II. They _____.

4. Martin sees words inside the ring. The _____ is small, but Martin can read it.

5. David's son doesn't pay Martin for the ring. It is a _____ from Martin.

3 COMPREHENSION

UNDERSTANDING SEQUENCE

Write the sentences in the correct order.

> Martin sends it to David's son.
> The Russian soldier gives it to a Hungarian woman.
> David's parents give him a gold ring.
> The Hungarian woman gives it to her grandson, Martin.
> David gives it to a Russian soldier.

1. David's parents give him a gold ring.
2. _____
3. _____
4. _____
5. _____

UNDERSTANDING PRONOUNS

Who is it? What is it? Write letter of your answer on the line.

_d_ 1. *They* give their son a gold ring.
____ 2. A Russian soldier gives *them* to David.
____ 3. *They* both survive the war.
____ 4. *She* gives food to the Russian soldier.
____ 5. *He* is the Hungarian woman's grandson.
____ 6. *He* is the U.S. soldier's son.
____ 7. *It* is a gift from Martin.

a. Martin
b. the gold ring
c. David C. Cox and the Russian soldier
d. David's parents
e. a Hungarian woman
f. two chocolate bars
g. David C. Cox, Jr.

4 DISCUSSION / WRITING

The soldier's son will give the gold ring to his children, and they will give it to their children. The ring will pass from generation to generation.

A What things do people in your country often pass from generation to generation? For example, do they pass jewelry, books, or a house? Complete the sentence below.

In my country, people often pass _____,

_____, and _____

from generation to generation.

B Share your sentence with the class.

The Gold Ring 81

KEY TO GUESSED ANSWERS

UNIT 5

DISCUSSION page 21

A There is about $200 dollars in the cash register. (There is usually more money in the store, but it is not in the cash register. It is in a safe.)

B The man is in prison from 3 to 7 years. If the man has a gun, he is in prison longer—from 5 to 10 years.

UNIT 9

DISCUSSION / WRITING page 37

A
1. On average, people in the United States go to the doctor four times a year.
2. People are with the doctor about 13 minutes.
3. The average doctor visit costs $160.
4. The average emergency room visit costs $1,233.

UNIT 19

DISCUSSION page 77

B The judge decided as follows:

the carpenter	20%	$30,000
Mr. Williams	40%	$60,000
Olga	40%	$60,000

DICTATION PREPARATION DIRECTIONS

To prepare for a dictation, follow these steps.

1. Look and listen as your teachers says the sentences and acts them out.
2. Act out the sentences with your teacher as your teacher says them.
3. Act out the sentences as your teacher says them. This time your teacher will not move.
4. Act out the sentences as your teacher says them. This time repeat the sentences after your teacher.
5. Repeat the sentences silently.

ANSWER KEY

UNIT 1

VOCABULARY   page 4
   2. drive away
   3. robber
   4. fix
   5. neighbor
   6. carry

REMEMBERING DETAILS   page 4
   2. b   3. b   4. a   5. a   6. b

REVIEWING THE STORY   page 5
   2. carrying
   3. repairmen
   4. TV
   5. robbers

UNIT 2

VOCABULARY   page 8
   2. top of the car
   3. wave
   4. turn left
   5. afraid
   6. follow

REMEMBERING DETAILS   page 8
   2. a   3. a   4. b   5. b

REVIEWING THE STORY   page 9
   2. afraid
   3. police
   4. officer
   5. There's
   6. gone

WRITING   page 9
   2. left, Park
   3. left, Sixth
   4. right, Street
   5. right

Answer Key   85

UNIT 3

VOCABULARY page 12
2. Venezuela
3. winner
4. lift weights
5. model

REMEMBERING DETAILS page 12
2. ~~intelligent~~ / beautiful
3. ~~children~~ / men
4. ~~doctor~~ / model
5. ~~pizza~~ / chicken
6. ~~meat~~ / candy

MAKING CONNECTIONS page 13
2. c   3. a   4. d

UNIT 4

VOCABULARY page 16
2. gloves
3. farmworker
4. berries
5. leaves
6. forest

FINDING INFORMATION pages 16–17
2. a forest
3. for two hours
4. better
5. he is sorry
6. he is lost
7. for one week
8. berries, leaves, and snow
9. on the cold ground
10. some farmworkers

UNDERSTANDING THE MAIN IDEAS page 17
2. a, c
3. a, b
4. b, c

UNIT 5

VOCABULARY   page 20
2. cashier
3. $20 bill
4. counter
5. pocket
6. bag

REMEMBERING DETAILS   page 20
2. a   3. b   4. b   5. a

REVIEWING THE STORY   page 21
2. opens
3. shows
4. money
5. all
6. store

UNIT 6

VOCABULARY   page 24
2. nice
3. hardworking
4. calls
5. pets
6. meets

UNDERSTANDING PRONOUNS   page 24
2. c   3. d   4. e   5. a

REMEMBERING DETAILS   page 24
2. not married
3. love
4. not happy
5. painter
6. WIFE
7. Hundreds

Answer Key   87

UNIT 7

VOCABULARY page 28
2. follow
3. curve
4. pull over
5. license
6. king

REMEMBERING DETAILS page 28
2. Norway
3. fast
4. ten kilometers over the speed limit
5. king of Norway

MAKING CONNECTIONS page 29
2. e   3. c   4. a   5. b

UNIT 8

VOCABULARY page 32
2. knock on doors
3. mail letters
4. give speeches
5. vote
6. call people on the phone

UNDERSTANDING THE MAIN IDEAS page 32
2. c   3. b

REMEMBERING DETAILS page 33
3. He puts up signs.
4. He calls people on the phone.
5. He mails letters.
7. He knocks on doors and talks to people.

UNIT 9

VOCABULARY page 36
2. hurts
3. limp
4. surgery
5. toward
6. dangerous

MAKING CONNECTIONS page 36

    2. f   3. c   4. b   5. d   6. a

REVIEWING THE STORY page 36

    2. still
    3. work
    4. bear
    5. building
    6. knee

UNIT 10

VOCABULARY page 40

    2. cheap
    3. fits
    4. counts
    5. owner

UNDERSTANDING THE MAIN IDEAS page 40

    2. shirt, large
    3. money
    4. days
    5. can't
    6. keep

FINDING MORE INFORMATION page 40

    2. d   3. a   4. c   5. e

UNIT 11

VOCABULARY page 44

    2. puppies
    3. worried
    4. locked
    5. fills
    6. cool

REMEMBERING DETAILS page 44

    2. hot summer day
    3. two puppies are in the car
    4. thirsty
    5. one hour
    6. police officer breaks a car window

UNDERSTANDING PRONOUNS page 45

    2. e   3. c   4. a   5. b

UNIT 12

VOCABULARY page 48
2. lessons
3. landing
4. practicing
5. noise
6. on top of

REMEMBERING DETAILS page 48
2. small airplane
3. on top of the small airplane
4. Sorry. I was landing, too. I didn't see you.
5. two airplanes

WHO SAYS IT? page 49
2. b   3. a   4. c

UNIT 13

VOCABULARY page 52
2. dump
3. town
4. lottery ticket
5. garbage can
6. garbage truck

REMEMBERING DETAILS page 52
2. a   3. b   4. b   5. a

LEARNING PAST TENSE FORMS page 53
2. win — won
3. throw — threw
4. come — came

UNIT 14

VOCABULARY page 56
2. behind
3. steering wheel
4. brake
5. passengers
6. hero

REMEMBERING DETAILS page 56

    2. b   3. b   4. b   5. b   6. a

UNDERSTANDING PRONOUNS page 57

    2. e   3. a   4. b   5. f   6. d

UNIT 15

VOCABULARY page 60

    2. lonely
    3. waitress
    4. kind
    5. calls
    6. check

UNDERSTANDING THE MAIN IDEAS page 60

    2. c   3. a

REMEMBERING DETAILS page 61

    2. b   3. a   4. a   5. b   6. b

UNIT 16

VOCABULARY page 64

    2. throat
    3. stuck
    4. breathe
    5. check

REMEMBERING DETAILS page 64

    2. ~~cake~~ / soup
    3. ~~fish~~ / chicken
    4. ~~potato~~ / rice
    5. ~~make~~ / eat
    6. ~~tooth~~ / throat
    7. ~~white~~ / purple
    8. ~~vegetables~~ / mochi

MAKING CONNECTIONS page 65

    2. d   3. a   4. b   5. c

UNIT 17

VOCABULARY page 68

7 games
3 plate
4 dirty socks
1 toys
5 fork
2 cookies
6 sofa

REMEMBERING DETAILS page 68

2. a   3. b   4. b   5. a

UNDERSTANDING PRONOUNS page 69

2. d   3. c   4. a

WRITING page 69

2. Rene is washing the dishes.
3. Rene is washing the clothes.
4. Rene is watching TV / Rene is sitting on the sofa.

UNIT 18

VOCABULARY page 72

2. ship
3. address
4. bottle
5. throw
6. sea

REMEMBERING DETAILS page 72

2. nothing to do
3. 18 years old
4. one year
5. English

MAKING CONNECTIONS page 73

2. c   3. a   4. b

UNIT 19

VOCABULARY page 76

2. ceiling
3. remodel
4. hires
5. found
6. judge

UNDERSTANDING THE MAIN IDEAS pages 76–77

2. a   3. a   4. b   5. a

WHO SAYS IT? page 77

2. b   3. c   4. a

UNIT 20

VOCABULARY page 80

2. prisoner
3. survive
4. writing
5. gift

UNDERSTANDING SEQUENCE page 80

2. David gives it to a Russian soldier.
3. The Russian soldier gives it to a Hungarian woman.
4. The Hungarian woman gives it to her grandson, Martin.
5. Martin sends it to David's son.

UNDERSTANDING PRONOUNS page 81

2. f   3. c   4. e   5. a   6. g   7. b

CREDITS

PHOTO CREDITS

Page 3: IS825/Image Source/Alamy Stock Photo; **7:** Kazbek Chermit/Shutterstock; **11:** David Ryo/Shutterstock; **15:** Crydo/Shutterstock; **17:** Fanfo/Shutterstock; **19:** Billion Photos/Shutterstock; **23:** Danm12/Shutterstock; **27:** Yauhen_D/Shutterstock; **31:** Hill Street Studios/Blend Images/Getty Images; **35:** Paul Knowles/Shutterstock; **39:** Shaffandi/123RF; **43:** Ed Fox/Aurora/Getty Images; **47:** Courtesy of Stanley Pure; **51:** Novak.elcic/Shutterstock; **55:** Al Schaben/Los Angeles Times/Getty Images; **59:** Dorota Magdziarz/Alamy Stock Photo; **63:** Iydiarei/Shutterstock; **67:** Jo Ann Snover/Shutterstock; **71:** Magnus Johansson/123RF; **75:** Alicia Ramirez/Shutterstock; **79:** PBO Photography/Shutterstock; **81:** Jr images/Shutterstock.